Daniel 11 and the Medieval Divided Kingdoms

The Struggle between Rome and Constantinople for Church-State Supremacy

by
Perry F. Louden, Jr. PhD

TEACH Services, Inc.
PUBLISHING
www.TEACHServices.com • (800) 367-1844

World rights reserved. This book or any portion thereof may not be copied or reproduced in any form or manner whatever, except as provided by law, without the written permission of the publisher, except by a reviewer who may quote brief passages in a review.

The author assumes full responsibility for the accuracy of all facts and quotations as cited in this book. The opinions expressed in this book are the author's personal views and interpretations, and do not necessarily reflect those of the publisher.

This book is provided with the understanding that the publisher is not engaged in giving spiritual, legal, medical, or other professional advice. If authoritative advice is needed, the reader should seek the counsel of a competent professional.

Copyright © 2021 Perry F. Louden, Jr. PhD
Copyright © 2021 TEACH Services, Inc.
ISBN-13: 978-1-4796-1331-1 (Paperback)
ISBN-13: 978-1-4796-1332-8 (ePub)
Library of Congress Control Number: 2021905374

Scripture quotations are from The ESV® Bible (The Holy Bible, English Standard Version®), copyright © 2001 by Crossway, a publishing ministry of Good News Publishers. Used by permission. All rights reserved.

> *"For such a time as this."*
> Mordecai to Queen Esther, c.a. 475 BC

> *"The light that Daniel received from God was given especially for these last days."*
> Ellen White—GW 113, 1896

> *"The world is stirred with the spirit of war. The prophecy of the eleventh chapter of Daniel has nearly reached its complete fulfillment. Soon the scenes of trouble spoken of in the prophecies will take place."*
> Ellen G. White—Testimonies Vol. 9, p 14, 1909

> *"I do not think we are through with this chapter [Daniel 11]. This is one of the great chapters [that] will be able to help men to see the hand of God is in human history."*
> Christian. M. Sorenson—SDA Bible Conference, 1919

> *"I have two fears in teaching. The first is that people will not believe me. My second is that they will without checking it out. Be like the Bereans.[1]"*
> Dr. Roy Gane—Daniel 11 Symposium 2018

---

[1] Roy Gane, "A Suggested Interpretation of Daniel 11:1–21," *American Christian Ministries,* n.d. Retrieved September 27, 2020, from https://1ref.us/1cy.

Table of Contents

Foreword 7
Chapter 1: Introduction 9
Chapter 2: Interpretation Methodology 12
Chapter 3: Prophecy of Daniel 10–12 16
Chapter 4: The Parallel Passages in Daniel 11 24
Chapter 5: Imperial Rome in Verses 20–22 29
Chapter 6: Interpretation of Verses 20–22 34
Chapter 7: Medieval Divided Kingdoms in Verses 23–39 37
Chapter 8: Historical Context of Daniel 11:23–39 43
       a.   Church-State Systems 44
       b.   Europe 47
       c.   Attacks on the Covenant 52
Chapter 9: Interpretation of Verses 23–39 59
       a.   Establishment of Church-State System 59
       b.   Protestant Revolution 78
       c.   Full Power and Authority of the Papacy 82
Chapter 10: End-Time Divided Kingdoms 85
Chapter 11: Ellen White and Daniel 11 87
Chapter 12: Conclusion 95
Appendix A Brief Verse by Verse Interpretation of Daniel 11 97
Appendix B The 21 Ecumenical Councils 109
Appendix C The Continual Sanctuary Ministry 115
Bibliography 120

Foreword

In his detailed study of Daniel 11, the author seeks to extend the thematic parallelism between Daniel 2, 7, 8 and 9 to Daniel 10–12. Drawing on well-established Adventist principles of interpretation and insights on Daniel 11 from the Spirit of Prophecy, the author proposes that Daniel 11 follows the well-established sequence of historical powers outlined in Daniel 2, 7 and 8. He argues that the common Adventist interpretation in which the narrative moves forward in time to the crucifixion in v. 22, only to then move back in time to the Maccabean alliance is without exegetical basis nor interpretive precedent within Daniel.

The author then provides a new interpretation of Daniel 11.23–29, arguing that this particular passage with its confrontation between the Kings of the North and the South represents the conflicts between the two competing and persecuting unions of church and state that followed imperial Rome, i.e. Papal Rome and Byzantium. This transition from imperial to papal Rome, and to a persecuting union of church and state in Daniel 11.23–29 mirrors the same sequencing of powers found in Daniel 2, 7 and 8. The author then moves to a commonly-held Adventist interpretation (particularly from the time of Louis Were onwards) for vv. 36–39, arguing that these verses represent the full flowering of papal arrogance and supremacy prior to the ending of the 1,260 year prophecy. Particularly insightful is how the author sequences verses 23–39 against the flow of chapters in *The Great Controversy between Christ and Satan* by Ellen G. White.

The author arrives at v. 40, interpreting (as do many Adventist interpreters) the time of the end as beginning at the end of the 1,260 year prophecy, i.e. in AD 1798, but the author does not provide a detailed analysis of the conflict between the Kings of the North or the South in vv.

40–45. While the identity of the KON is clear (papal Rome, backed by the military might of the West in general and the USA in particular), the identity of the KOS remains more obscure, although the author does indicate provisional backing for the atheism interpretation held commonly among Adventists since the writings of Louis Were and Dr. Hans LaRondelle. Detailed appendices provide helpful interpretive information to guide the reader in further study.

Throughout the book, the author seeks to follow well-established Adventist principles of interpretation (which he helpfully outlines early on) and a brief but detailed analysis of the commentary found in the Spirit of Prophecy. He builds his case on the well-established portrayal of a persecuting union of church and state that would arise after pagan Rome in Daniel 2, 7 and 8. This approach lends credibility to the conclusions relating to the identities of the KON and the KOS in 11.23–39. Further work is required however to identify how and if the KOS in vv.40–45 is also a persecuting union of church of state, or a secular equivalent, if the well-established patterns found earlier in Daniel are to be continued throughout Daniel 11. This book is a welcome and insightful addition to the ongoing prayerful reflection on this critical portion of eschatological prophecy within the wider SDA community.

Dr. Conrad Vine
President, Adventist Frontier Missions, Inc. (www.afmonline.org)

Chapter 1:
Introduction

In my early twenties, I was in the Army Reserve and had to get a haircut before a weekend drill. Being on my own and not having much money, I would get my haircuts at a barber school and then just pay the student hairstylist a tip. I noticed the stylist-in-training would cut one side, then the back, then the other side, and then the top. He finished, and I thought it looked great, but the instructor came over to check it. He did not go around the sides, then the top. He started on one side of my forehead and worked back to the opposite side; then, he started on the opposite side and went back, making an X across the top of my head in a crisscross shape. I could not believe how much hair was missed by the student-stylist!

In the same way, we generally study the book of Daniel chapter by chapter. While we can learn much from that technique, we can also "run to and fro" in the book and increase our knowledge and understanding by studying the book of Daniel chronologically—empire by empire across the four prophecies. When studying and teaching Daniel chapter by chapter, we are continually backing up and reviewing what came before to understand the chapter we are focusing on. Yet, when looking at the prophecies chronologically, we can gain amazing insights and understandings with a fuller presentation of each kingdom and that period. My original goal was to learn more about Daniel and possibly create a new Bible study series on Daniel for non-Seventh-day Adventists. My study resulted in a new position to interpret verses 23 to 39—The Rome and Constantinople position.

The Book of Daniel is the reason the Seventh-day Adventist Church exists today since our early pioneers pored over Daniel 2, 7, 8, and 9 with eagerness, vigor, and gusto! They did the heavy lifting on the interpretation of Daniel's prophecies, and they left only a small portion in Chapter 11 without a concise, succinct, and clear interpretation. For over 175 years, Seventh-day Adventist ministers, evangelists, and even lay workers have powerfully preached the message of hope in the judgment found in the prophecies of Daniel 2, 7, 8, and 9. Even so, the prophecy and message of Daniel 11 remain largely obscure to the vast number of Seventh-day Adventists and that eagerness, vigor, and gusto are strikingly lacking in our presentations of this portion of Daniel that built our church.

> *The prophecy and message of Daniel 11 remain largely obscure to the vast number of Seventh-day Adventists and that eagerness, vigor, and gusto are strikingly lacking in our presentations of this portion of Daniel that built our church.*

What follows is a preliminary position of Daniel 11 that came out of a study on Daniel chronologically—empire by empire—and not our usual chapter by chapter study. This method of studying kingdom by kingdom worked well for the first four empires, and one can easily see the start and end of Babylon, Medo-Persia, Greece, and Rome in chapters 2, 7, 8, 9, and even in chapter 11. However, the divided kingdoms were missing or obscured in Daniel 11. After checking commentaries, Adventists scholars, and doing online research, I discovered no clear agreement in our church on this portion of Scripture. Through much prayer and diligent study, I discovered a parallel to Daniel 2 in Daniel 11. This study in the following pages will explore those parallels.

This position is by no means meant to be the end-all to our study and dialogue on Daniel 11. While I stand by the overall thesis presented here, scholars' refinement in the area of biblical research and history may be needed to comb through and make changes where necessary to the position. The result must be to put an end to our vacillation among a multitude of positions and opinions in Daniel 11. We are in the toenails of Daniel's Image, and we must present all Daniel's prophecies with the same power and exuberance of those giving the message of hope in the judgment before October 22, 1844.

Before moving on to the study, I would like to address briefly two vital principles: first, the separation of church and state, second, individual freedom of conscience. The former we have today because the Founders of our great nation placed this principle at the very onset of the U.S. Constitution. The latter was handed down to us by the Protestant Reformers, who gave their blood to wrestle this from the church-state power of their time. Both principles are under assault today. Our Protestant Founders established a religious nation based on Judeo-Christian principles, where all people could follow the dictates of their conscience. However, many today want to see our nation become the 21st century Christendom. We must, and are instructed to, raise our voices against this movement, pointing to the horrific past record. At the same time, we must encourage others, with love and long-suffering, to search the Scriptures for themselves and act upon their individual consciences. Ms. Nancy, a wise lady from our church who is now resting in Jesus, once said, "Others may, but I may not," and that is the essence of freedom of conscience.

> *The result must be to put an end to our vacillation among a multitude of positions and opinions in Daniel 11. We are in the toenails of Daniel's Image, and we must present all Daniel's prophecies with the same power and exuberance of those giving the message of hope in the judgment before October 22, 1844.*

Spoiler Alert

Here is a brief outline of the proposed interpretation of Daniel 11:

Verse(s)	Empire/Power
11:2	Medo-Persia
11:3–19	Greece with Hellenistic Dynasties of the Seleucids and Ptolemy
11:20–22	Imperial Rome
11:23–39	Medieval Divided Kingdoms with Church-State Systems of Rome and Constantinople
11:40–45	End-Time Divided Kingdoms
12:1	Michael delivers His people

The remainder of this book will give the reasoning behind this interpretation.

Chapter 2:
Interpretation Methodology

Consistent principles of interpretation are the hallmark of successfully understanding the message God has for us in prophecy. The positions set forth are predicated on time-tested Adventist methods of biblical interpretation.

> *Consistent principles of interpretation are the hallmark of successfully understanding the message God has for us in prophecy.*

Parallel Prophecies

Daniel crafts his prophecies in parallels which are seen throughout his book. Chapters 2 and 7, written predominately in Aramaic, parallel each other and discuss secular world empires. The prophecies in chapters 8–9 and 10–12 again parallel each other and discuss the sanctuary ministry and the covenant. Unlike the prophecies in chapters 2 and 7, these final two prophecies were written predominately in Hebrew.

Observations on the four prophecies of Daniel

Several observations are apparent in the four main prophecies. First, the prophecies in Daniel 2 and 7 focus on the beginning and end of each empire with characteristics and generalities about the empire occurring within their reign. Next, the prophecy in Daniel 8–9 focuses on God's people, the temple, and the Sanctuary service which is crucial to understanding Daniel 10–12. Finally, the prophecy of Daniel 10–12 focuses on the overall shifts in the balance of power (not necessarily the end of the kingdom) and on how kings and kingdoms affect God's people and the ministry of the temple.

Daniel 2 Political Divisions

We often see Nebuchadnezzar's image as having five political divisions — 1) head, 2) chest and arms, 3) belly and thighs, 4) legs, and 5) feet and toes. Yet, there are actually 6 divisions in Daniel 2. Notice the distinction between feet and the toes found in verses 41–42, "And as you saw the **feet and toes**, partly of potter's clay and partly of iron, it shall be a divided kingdom, but some of the firmness of iron shall be in it, just as you saw iron mixed with the soft clay. And as the **toes of the feet** were partly iron and partly clay, so the kingdom shall be partly strong and partly brittle."

Our six political divisions are as follows:

Head	Babylon	605 BC–538 BC
Chest and Arms	Medo-Persia	538 BC–331 BC
Belly and Thighs	Greece	331 BC–31 BC
Legs	Rome	31 BC–AD 476
Feet	Medieval Divided Kingdoms	AD 476–1798
Toes	End-Time Divided Kingdoms	1798–2nd Coming

These six political divisions and time periods will guide us throughout the remaining three prophecies in Daniel. How that breaks down, verse by verse, is seen in the following chart:

Prophecy Divisions by Empire

Empire	2	7	8–9	10–12
Babylon	32, 37–38	4, 12, 17	n/a	n/a
Medo-Persia	32, 39	5, 12, 17	8:3, 4, 14, 20, 26; 9:23–25	2
Greece	32, 39	6, 12, 17	8:6–8, 21–22	3–19
Rome	33, 40	7, 12, 17, 19, 23	8:9, 10a, 23;* 9:26, 27a	20–22
Medieval Divided Kingdoms	33b, 41–43	8, 20–21, 24–25	8:10–14, 23–26; 9:27c	23–39
End-Time Divided Kingdoms	43, 42, 44	9–11, 22, 26, 27	25	40–45

*Rome and Medieval Divided Kingdoms are mingled in these verses.

Rules for Interpretation

Rules for interpretation of the book of Daniel have been passed down to us from the church pioneers and are of preeminence for understanding the message God has for us in these prophecies. For this study these rules include: 1) using Daniel chapter 2 as the template for the understanding the other three prophecies in the book of Daniel; 2) understanding that prophecies are repeated and enlarged upon; and 3) allowing the Bible to interpret itself by using the immediate context first, then moving out to surrounding passages, the rest of the book, and finally, to the whole Bible, especially any words of Jesus which may apply.

Having established consistent and time-tested rules for interpretation, we can now move to our main focus of the longest of Daniel's prophecies found in chapters 10–12 and specifically chapter 11. One might ask, what about the prophecies found in chapters 7–9? There is virtually universal agreement in the Seventh-day Adventist Church over the general interpretation of these prophecies. If you would like to learn more about these, the *Seventh-day Adventist Bible Commentary Volume 4* has abundant material on the book of Daniel, or you may also check with the Adventist Book Center.

Interpretation Methodology 15

Stages of Prophetic History

1. Babylonian Empire (605 - 539BC)

Daniel 2	Daniel 7	Daniel 8-9	Daniel 10-12
		N/A	N/A

2. Medo-Persian Empire (539 - 331BC)

Daniel 2	Daniel 7	Daniel 8-9	Daniel 10-12
			Cyrus Delivers God's People

3. Greek Empire (331 - 31BC)

Daniel 2	Daniel 7	Daniel 8-9	Daniel 10-12
			KON - Seleucid Dynasty KOS - Ptolemaic Dynasty

4. Roman Empire (31BC - 476 AD)

Daniel 2	Daniel 7	Daniel 8-9	Daniel 10-12
			Literal Rome arises and destroys the Prince of the Covenant

5. Medieval Divided Kingdoms (476 - 1798)

Daniel 2	Daniel 7	Daniel 8-9	Daniel 10-12
			KON – Rome Church-State Union KOS – Constantinople Church-State Union

6. End-Time Divided Kingdoms (1798 - 2nd Coming)

Daniel 2	Daniel 7	Daniel 8-9	Daniel 10-12
			Spiritual Rome attempts to destroy the People of the Covenant

7. God's Eternal Kingdom

Daniel 2	Daniel 7	Daniel 8-9	Daniel 10-12
			Michael Delivers God's People

Chapter 3:

Prophecy of Daniel 10–12

Introduction to the Prophecy of Daniel 10–12

We read in Daniel 10:1, "In the third year of Cyrus king of Persia a word was revealed to Daniel, who was named Belteshazzar. And the word was true, and it was a great conflict. And he understood the word and had understanding of the vision."

The prophecy of chapters 10–12 begins with Daniel praying and mourning for his people and is told by the angel the prophecy is a great battle or conflict. Daniel 11 is about great battles/conflicts centered around God's people. There are two key questions we need to ask: 1) What are these great battles/conflicts? and 2) Where do we find God's People during these conflicts?

We can understand Daniel 11 based on previous prophecies using the repeat and enlarge principles. Consider the statement, "He (Daniel) understood the word and had understanding of the vision." Daniel explicitly states he understood the vision in chapter 11. However, in Daniel 8, we found that he did not understand that vision and needed more explanation which is found in Chapter 9. In chapter 8 and verse 27 we read, "And I, Daniel, was overcome and lay sick for some days. Then I rose and went about the king's business, but **I was appalled by the vision and did not understand it.**" In Daniel 9:22 we read, "He made me understand, speaking with me and saying, "O Daniel, **I have now come out to give you insight and understanding.**" Why would Daniel be able to understand this vision in Daniel 11– that we have such a hard time understanding – but he could not understand about the 2300 days which is the basis for our existence as Seventh-day Adventists? The answer lies in chapter 8 where

Daniel understands what is called the *chazown* section of the vision which he had already seen in Daniel 2 and 7, but what is called the *mar'eh* vision portion he doesn't understand because it was not in Daniel 2 and 7. We also see Daniel asking for understanding about the "time, times, and half a time" in chapter 12 verses 7 and 8. The only conclusion is that Daniel 11 must be a repetition and enlargement of what Daniel saw in the visions of 2, 7, and 8–9. Nothing can be added in chapter 11 or Daniel would not have understood it. Themes in Revelation, while they are certainly true and may fit perfectly into Daniel's four prophecies, cannot be interjected into Daniel 11. Daniel would undoubtedly have asked the angel for an explanation.

This vision in chapters 10–12 is for us in the latter days. The angel states in 10:14 that he came "to make you (Daniel) understand what is to happen to your people in the **latter days.** For the vision is **for days yet to come.**" If the vision of great struggles is about the end of time, why did the angel spend so much time on the Kings of the North and South during the Greek empire? The answer must be that verses 4–19 can help us to interpret the parallel verses of 23–39.

> *Themes in Revelation, while they are certainly true and may fit perfectly into Daniel's four prophecies, cannot be interjected into Daniel 11.*

Guidelines for the Interpretation of Daniel 11

Daniel 11 presents some unique challenges for interpretation that we must take into consideration for proper understanding. While some texts have incredible detail, others exhibit an extreme amount of obscurity. Take verse 23 for example: "And from the time (what time?) that an alliance (which alliance?) is made with him (who?) he (who?) shall act deceitfully, and he (which he?) shall become strong with a small people (Romans? Jews? someone else?)." For this verse and many like it, the old adage of context is king must be applied.

While some passages are obscure, we do know without a doubt that Jesus is at the center of Daniel 11. We read in verse 22, "Armies shall be utterly swept away before him and broken, **even the prince of the covenant.**" Just as Jesus is Messiah (anointed one) the Prince in Daniel 9:25, we see Jesus here as the true Prince of the Covenant. Before verse 22, the focus is on God's people in the physical Jewish nation while after verse 22 the focus is on God's spiritual Jews in the Christian church.[1]

---
1 See Rom. 2:28–29.

Another unique aspect of Daniel 11 is the kings and kingdoms end when their authority and/or power is superseded by other kings or kingdoms coming on the scene. In verse 2 we read, "Behold, three more kings shall arise in Persia, and a fourth (Xerxes I) shall be far richer than all of them. And when he has become strong through his riches, he shall stir up all against the kingdom of Greece." Xerxes lost to the Greeks at the Battles of Salamis and Plataea in ca. 480 BC and the power shifted to Greece even though seven more kings reigned in Medo-Persia. This differs from the previous prophecies in chapters 2 and 7 where the kingdoms end completely, and the new kingdom begins.

Daniel 11 has several compass texts. These are texts which give us a sense of location and direction in the chapter. A verse from the prophecy may fit its historical situation nearly perfectly as we see in verse 5, "Then the king of the south (Ptolemy I Soter) shall be strong, but one of his princes (Seleucus Nicator) shall be stronger than he and shall rule, and his authority shall be a great authority."[2] We can also see compass texts in the phrase "do as he wills" designating a new king has arisen. We read in verse 3, "Then a mighty king (Alexander the Great) shall arise, who shall rule with great dominion and do as he wills."

Now let us look at the comparison of empire collapses in Daniel 2 and 7 with Daniel 11. The former gives the total collapse of the empire while the latter gives the rise of the next dominant power. We can visualize this in the following graph:

Empire	Beginning in Daniel 2 & 7	End in Daniel 11	End in Daniel 2 & 7
Babylon	605 BC	n/a	539 BC Cyrus conquers Babylon
Medo-Persia	539 BC	480 BC Battle of Thermopylae	331 BC Battle of Gaugamela
Greece	331 BC	188 BC Treaty of Apamea[3]	31 BC Battle of Actium
Rome	168 BC	AD 31 Prince of the Covenant is crucified	AD 476 Barbarian king Odoacer deposed the Roman emperor

---

2 The Seleucid kingdom became much larger and more powerful than the Ptolemaic kingdom.
3 H. Volkmann, "Antiochus III the Great," Britannica, 2019. Retrieved September 27, 2020, from https://1ref.us/143.

Empire	Beginning in Daniel 2 & 7	End in Daniel 11	End in Daniel 2 & 7
Medieval Divided Kingdoms	AD 476	1798 Conquered by France	1798 Conquered by France
End-Time Divided Kingdoms	1798	People of the Prince Delivered	2nd Coming

In Daniel 8, we get a clarification as to why there is a gap between the new power arising on the scene while the old power declines over time. We read in Daniel 7:12, "As for the rest of the beasts, their dominion was taken away, but their lives were prolonged for a season and a time." However, the previous verse is explicit in that Papal Rome is the exception, going to the end of time and then ends immediately just before the 2nd Coming. Verse 11, "I looked then because of the sound of the great words that the horn was speaking. And as I looked, the beast was killed, and its body destroyed and given over to be burned with fire."

Michael, Lucifer, and Antiochus IV

Before we move into the specific interpretation of Daniel 11, we need to understand three names involved in clearly seeing God's purpose and message for us. Here we have the good, the bad, and ugly, respectively, Michael, Lucifer, and Antiochus IV. Michael, the good one, is visibly working on behalf of His people to influence leaders. Lucifer, the bad one, is not mentioned in the text but is noticeably active behind the scenes and attempting to corrupt God's people. We also have Antiochus IV Epiphanes, the ugly one, who by all outside accounts was appalling and horrifying yet his kingship did not rise to Daniel's standard for being part of the "great conflict" which we find in Daniel 11.

Who Is Michael of Daniel 10–12?

Michael, as a heavenly being is mentioned three times in Daniel's vision in chapters 10–12. He is also mentioned twice in the New Testament: once in Jude 9 where He is disputing with Satan over the resurrection of Moses to heaven and another in Revelation 12 where He is commanding the war in heaven against Satan and his angels.

There are three views on who Michael is. The first is held by most of the Christian world where Michael is the highest, or Archangel,[4] and one of

---
4   Jude 9.

the chief princes,[5] with Gabriel being subordinate to Him. The second view is held by Jehovah's Witnesses where Michael is Jesus, a created being, and is the brother of Lucifer. Lucifer rebelled and the Father sent Michael (Jesus) to die on the cross and defeat Lucifer there. The third position is held by Adventists where Michael is the pre-incarnate Jesus, one with the Father before the incarnation and fully God and fully man after the incarnation. The following reasons for this position are outlined here:

1. The name Michael in Hebrew means "who is like God." No one other than Jesus is like God the Father. John 10:30, "I and the Father are one."

2. The word Archangel is from two words, arch meaning "chief" and angel meaning "messenger." John states in 1:1–2, "In the beginning was the Word, and the Word was with God, and the Word was God. He was in the beginning with God." From Strong's Definition:

    > λόγος lógos, log'-os; from G3004; something said (including the thought); by implication, a topic (subject of discourse), also reasoning (the mental faculty) or motive; by extension, a computation; specially, (with the article in John) the Divine Expression (i.e. Christ):—account, cause, communication.

    Therefore, Jesus' role in the trinity is that of the chief messenger to both angels and humankind.

3. In Daniel 10:13, the angel Gabriel could not influence the king of Persia because Satan was influencing the king. Michael had to come and influence the king of Persia. Gabriel, as the highest angel, can influence humans and is tasked with vital messages to give to humans like Daniel[6] and Mary the mother of Jesus.[7] He has no power against Satan. "Are they (angels) not all ministering spirits sent out to serve for the sake of those who are to inherit salvation?"[8]

4. Young's Literal Translation Bible (YLT) translates the phrase in Daniel 10:13b as: "Michael, first of the chief heads" instead of: "one of the chief princes." Jesus is the chief or head of the angelic force. Jesus said in Matthew 13: 41, "The Son of Man (Jesus) will send his angels."

---

5 Dan. 10:13.
6 Dan. 8:16; 9:20–21.
7 Luke 1:19.
8 Heb. 1:14.

5. In both New Testament passages, Michael is fighting Satan. Only Jesus can defeat Satan. "He (Jesus) himself likewise partook of the same things, that through death he might destroy the one who has the power of death, that is, the devil, and deliver all those who through fear of death were subject to lifelong slavery."[9]

6. In Revelation 12, Michael fights and defeats Satan. He casts him out of heaven. Jesus plainly states in Luke 10:18, "And he said to them, 'I saw Satan fall like lightning from heaven.'"

7. The book of Daniel is about judgment and this is precisely what happens at the end of the prophecy in chapter 7. Daniel 12:1 states, "At that time shall arise Michael," however, the YLT is more accurate here with, "And at that time doth stand up Michael," or as we would say, "At that time Michael will stand up."

8. During a criminal trial, the judge sits while he or she listens to arguments from both sides. At the end of a court session, the judge makes his decision and stands up signifying the judgment is over and the decision is made. That is what is happening in Daniel 12: Michael has made his judgment against the King of the North and for His people and so he stands. Jesus said in John 5:22, "For the Father judgeth no man, but hath committed all judgment unto the Son." Judgment is never given to a mere angel; therefore, Michael here must be Jesus. We have more evidence in that when Stephen was being stoned in Acts chapter 7, Stephen has a vision while they are stoning him. Acts 7:56 states, "And he said, 'Behold, I see the heavens opened, and the Son of Man standing at the right hand of God.'" Here we see the conclusion of the 70 Weeks prophecy of Daniel 9 being fulfilled. The Jews were given 490 years (70 weeks) of probation and were found guilty of rejecting God by stoning His prophets, crucifying Christ, and finally stoning the final message, Stephen, to the Jewish people. Jesus has judged them guilty and has stood up.

For these reasons, we must conclude that Michael is the pre-incarnate Jesus. He is not a mere angel or a created being and brother of Lucifer. He is in fact the exact character and substance as the Father.

---

[9] Heb. 1:1–15.

Lucifer, the Real Power behind Earthly Empires

> *He is not a mere angel or a created being and brother of Lucifer. He is in fact the exact character and substance as the Father*

We do not find Lucifer, Satan, or the devil mentioned in Daniel; even so, we know clearly from Isaiah 14 the power behind Babylon, and, hence, all worldly powers, is indeed Lucifer, the son of the morning. This is representative of all worldly kingdoms except for Persia and King Cyrus who is a type of Michael's kingdom and deliverer in the prophecy of Daniel 10–12. The power behind the King of Persia is God. In Daniel 10:13 we read, "The prince of the kingdom of Persia withstood me twenty-one days, but Michael, one of the chief princes, came to help me, for I was left there with the kings of Persia." The exiles returned home under the decrees of Persia in a time of peace with the protection and authority of the power of the day. Their conflict was with the small nations around them who harassed them, but when they believed the promises of God, they were able to overcome these trials through God's strength.

All the kingdoms of this world including Greece, Imperial Rome, the medieval divided kingdoms, and the end-time divided kingdoms have had Satan behind them, and, as such, God's people must be vigilant against the actions Satan will use in the name of the state. After all, it was Satan who conspired with the Jewish Sanhedrin and the Roman authorities in a church-state union to crucify Jesus, the Prince of the Covenant; similarly, Satan will inspire papal–led Christianity and the United States to enforce a death decree on God's people at the end of time.

While Jesus ministers in the Most Holy Place in the heavenly sanctuary, we, God's people, must hold to the promises and exercise our duties as *Priests of the Lord*,[10] ministering in the Holy Place of the sanctuary. Priestly duties include ministering in the first compartment at the Table of Showbread with Bible study, at the altar of incense with our prayers to God, at the Lampstand and allowing our light to shine through our Fruit of the Spirit and Gifts, and always looking towards the Most Holy Place where the Ark of His Covenant is placed by accepting His mercy and emulating the character of Jesus through the keeping His Commandments.

---

10 1 Peter 2:9.

What about Antiochus IV Epiphanes?

Antiochus IV Epiphanes reigned from 175–164 BC and was a Seleucid king. Many in the Christian community feel he fulfilled the prophecies of the little horn in chapter 7 and was one of the Kings of the North in Daniel 11. Below are five reasons why Antiochus IV Epiphanes cannot be the King of the North found in Daniel 11.

1. In chapter 2, the nation after Greece was Rome, and the prophecies in 7, 8–9, and 10–11 have parallel kingdoms of chapter 2.
2. In chapter 7, the Little Horn came up out of the 10 and therefore is the 11th horn. Antiochus was, in reality, the 8th king of Greek Seleucid kingdom.
3. In chapter 8, Medo-Persia was "great"(v. 4), Greece was "very great" (v. 8), and the next kingdom is "exceeding great" (v. 9), yet Antiochus inherited his kingdom from his father and was stopped from expanding it into Egypt by the Roman Counsel in 168 BC and therefore never became "exceedingly great."
4. The horn in chapter 8 came up out of one of the winds, specifically the west wind, where the Greek empire had not reached. Antiochus came out of one of the "four conspicuous horns" from Alexander's empire.
5. He reigned during the Seleucid Empire period from 175 BC until he died in 164 BC, yet Jesus said, "So when you see the abomination of desolation spoken of by the prophet Daniel, standing in the holy place (let the reader understand), then let those who are in Judea flee to the mountains."[11] This did not occur until AD 70, over 234 years after his death.

To summarize, in the book of Daniel we see Jesus, as Michael, working on behalf of His people even to the point of death. However, Satan is always working behind the scenes through his surrogates to destroy the relationship Jesus has with his people. While Antiochus Epiphanies is certainly one of Satan's surrogate rulers, his short reign of 12 years hardly fits Daniel's criteria of "exceedingly great" and therefore not found in Daniel 11 as the King of the North.

---

11   Matt. 24:15, 16.

Chapter 4:
The Parallel Passages in Daniel 11

Daniel 11 has three sets of parallel verses which we can see as follows:

a) Medo-Persia/Everlasting Kingdom—Here we have two deliverers in Cyrus and Michael. Isaiah 45:1 indicates that Cyrus was a type of Christ or Michael, "Thus says the Lord to his anointed, to Cyrus, whose right hand I have grasped, to subdue nations before him and to loose the belts of kings, to open doors before him that gates may not be closed."

b) Greece/Medieval Divided Kingdoms—Here we have great kings who die in Alexander and Constantine and leave a power vacuum between the Kings of the North and the Kings of the South.

c) Imperial Rome/End-Time Divided Kingdoms—Here we have a church-state death decree for the Prince of the Covenant and the People of the Covenant.

Below is a comparison chart:

Medo-Persia verse 11:2 – Cyrus was the deliverer from literal Babylon to usher in time of peace with no KON or KOS

    Greece verses 3-19 on – KON Seleucids and KOS Ptolemy Dynasties

        Imperial Rome verses 20-22 on – *Kills the Prince of the Covenant*

        Divided Kingdoms verses 23-39 – KON and KOS Church/State Systems

            Papal Rome (Toes) verses 40-45 – *Attempts to kill the People of Covenant*

Everlasting Kingdoms verse 12:1 – Michael will be the deliverer from spiritual Babylon and usher in a time of peace with no KON or KOS

These parallel passages help to keep the interpretation on track by identifying similar keywords in the equivalent text. We apply these passages by detecting similar elements such as the "king of the south" (vv. 5 and 25) or we can see opposite elements with "mighty" (v. 3) and "deceitful" (v. 23). Additionally, the verse may be superseded by a prophetic element as with Cyrus and Michael (vv. 11:2 and 12:1). Even so, texts referring to the parallel kingdom must not supplant the meaning of the primary kingdom's interpretation. The parallel text acts as our guard rail beside the road; we drive on the paved road between the lines and only need the guard rail to prevent us from going in the ditch.

Even so, texts referring to the parallel kingdom must not supplant the meaning of the primary kingdom's interpretation.

While not intended to be a rigid, exegetical critique of the parallels in the Hebrew text, below we see a loose layout of these parallel passages:

Cyrus the Great and Deliverer	Michael the Prince and Deliverer
11:2 And now I will show you the truth. Behold, three more kings shall arise in Persia, and a fourth shall be far richer than all of them. And when he has become strong through his riches, he shall stir up all against the kingdom of Greece.	12:1 At that time shall arise Michael, the great prince who has charge of your people. And there shall be a time of trouble, such as never has been since there was a nation till that time. But at that time your people shall be delivered, everyone whose name shall be found written in the book.
Mighty King, KON and KOS	**Deceitful King, KON and KOS**
11:3 Then a mighty king shall arise, who shall rule with great dominion and do as he wills.	11:23 And from the time that an alliance is made with him he shall act deceitfully, and he shall become strong with a small people.
4 And as soon as he has arisen, his kingdom shall be broken and divided toward the four winds of heaven, but not to his posterity, nor according to the authority with which he ruled, for his kingdom shall be plucked up and go to others besides these.	24 Without warning he shall come into the richest parts[e] of the province, and he shall do what neither his fathers nor his fathers' fathers have done, scattering among them plunder, spoil, and goods. He shall devise plans against strongholds, but only for a time.

5 Then the king of the south shall be strong, but one of his princes shall be stronger than he and shall rule, and his authority shall be a great authority.	25a And he shall stir up his power and his heart against the king of the south with a great army.
6a After some years they shall make an alliance, and the daughter of the king of the south shall come to the king of the north to make an agreement.	25b And the king of the south shall wage war with an exceedingly great and mighty army, but he shall not stand, for plots shall be devised against him.
6b But she shall not retain the strength of her arm, and he and his arm shall not endure, but she shall be given up, and her attendants, he who fathered her, and he who supported her in those times.	26 Even those who eat his food shall break him. His army shall be swept away, and many shall fall down slain.
7 And from a branch from her roots one shall arise in his place. He shall come against the army and enter the fortress of the king of the north, and he shall deal with them and shall prevail.	27 And as for the two kings, their hearts shall be bent on doing evil. They shall speak lies at the same table, but to no avail, for the end is yet to be at the time appointed.
8 He shall also carry off to Egypt their gods with their metal images and their precious vessels of silver and gold, and for some years he shall refrain from attacking the king of the north.	28 And he shall return to his land with great wealth, but his heart shall be set against the holy covenant. And he shall work his will and return to his own land.
9 Then the latter shall come into the realm of the king of the south but shall return to his own land.	29 At the time appointed he shall return and come into the south, but it shall not be this time as it was before.
10 His sons shall wage war and assemble a multitude of great forces, which shall keep coming and overflow and pass through, and again shall carry the war as far as his fortress.	30 For ships of Kittim shall come against him, and he shall be afraid and withdraw, and shall turn back and be enraged and take action against the holy covenant. He shall turn back and pay attention to those who forsake the holy covenant.
11 Then the king of the south, moved with rage, shall come out and fight against the king of the north. And he shall raise a great multitude, but it shall be given into his hand.	31 Forces from him shall appear and profane the temple and fortress, and shall take away the regular burnt offering. And they shall set up the abomination that makes desolate.
12 And when the multitude is taken away, his heart shall be exalted, and he shall cast down tens of thousands, but he shall not prevail.	32 He shall seduce with flattery those who violate the covenant, but the people who know their God shall stand firm and take action.

The Parallel Passages in Daniel 11

13 For the king of the north shall again raise a multitude, greater than the first. And after some years he shall come on with a great army and abundant supplies.	33 And the wise among the people shall make many understand, though for some days they shall stumble by sword and flame, by captivity and plunder.
14 In those times many shall rise against the king of the south, and the violent among your own people shall lift themselves up in order to fulfill the vision, but they shall fail.	34 When they stumble, they shall receive a little help. And many shall join themselves to them with flattery,
15 Then the king of the north shall come and throw up siegeworks and take a well-fortified city. And the forces of the south shall not stand, or even his best troops, for there shall be no strength to stand.	35 and some of the wise shall stumble, so that they may be refined, purified, and made white, until the time of the end, for it still awaits the appointed time.
16 But he who comes against him shall do as he wills, and none shall stand before him. And he shall stand in the glorious land, with destruction in his hand.	36 And the king shall do as he wills. He shall exalt himself and magnify himself above every god, and shall speak astonishing things against the God of gods. He shall prosper till the indignation is accomplished; for what is decreed shall be done.
17 He shall set his face to come with the strength of his whole kingdom, and he shall bring terms of an agreement and perform them. He shall give him the daughter of women to destroy the kingdom, but it shall not stand or be to his advantage.	37 He shall pay no attention to the gods of his fathers, or to the one beloved by women. He shall not pay attention to any other god, for he shall magnify himself above all.
18 Afterward he shall turn his face to the coastlands and shall capture many of them, but a commander shall put an end to his insolence. Indeed, he shall turn his insolence back upon him.	38 He shall honor the god of fortresses instead of these. A god whom his fathers did not know he shall honor with gold and silver, with precious stones and costly gifts.
19 Then he shall turn his face back toward the fortresses of his own land, but he shall stumble and fall, and shall not be found.	39 He shall deal with the strongest fortresses with the help of a foreign god. Those who acknowledge him he shall load with honor. He shall make them rulers over many and shall divide the land for a price.

Imperial Rome arises and destroys the Prince of the Covenant	**Papal Rome arises and attempts to destroy the People of the Covenant**
11:20 Then shall arise in his place one who shall send an exactor of tribute for the glory of the kingdom. But within a few days he shall be broken, neither in anger nor in battle.	11:40 At the time of the end, the king of the south shall attack him, but the king of the north shall rush upon him like a whirlwind, with chariots and horsemen, and with many ships. And he shall come into countries and shall overflow and pass through.
21 In his place shall arise a contemptible person to whom royal majesty has not been given. He shall come in without warning and obtain the kingdom by flatteries.	41 He shall come into the glorious land. And tens of thousands shall fall, but these shall be delivered out of his hand: Edom and Moab and the main part of the Ammonites.
	42 He shall stretch out his hand against the countries, and the land of Egypt shall not escape.
	43 He shall become ruler of the treasures of gold and of silver, and all the precious things of Egypt, and the Libyans and the Cushites shall follow in his train.
22 Armies shall be utterly swept away before him and broken, even the prince of the covenant.	44 But news from the east and the north shall alarm him, and he shall go out with great fury to destroy and devote many to destruction.
	45 And he shall pitch his palatial tents between the sea and the glorious holy mountain. Yet he shall come to his end, with none to help him.

Chapter 5:
Rome in Verses 20–22

The proposition outlined here is that Imperial Rome constitutes only three verses. Even so, the predominant Seventh-day Adventist view is that Imperial Rome goes on through verse 29. There were issues that puzzled me regarding the historical/predominant view which led me to do more research and hunt for a better position.

1) When reading this section in the *SDA Bible Commentary, Vol 4*, it was quite evident that Seventh-day Adventists have had no consistent, unified view of the interpretation of these verses. The Commentary is continually citing two or three views per text.

2) Everything up to verse 22, including the prophecies in chapters 2, 7, and 8–9, are in chronological order. Why would Daniel suddenly say, "Oh, wait, I need to back up and add something"? In verse 23, many see this as the league or alliance between the Romans and the Jews 161 BC, yet if this is the case, the chapter has gone from AD 33/AD 70 in verse 22 back 194/231 years in verse 23. Daniel is meticulous in his prophetic detail and writing style, and his prophecies are always progressive in time and never regressive.

3) Next, there is historical information added in verses 23–29 that do not fit into Daniel's theme for the chapter of being a "great conflict" centered around God's people. In verses 24–27, many see the Battle of Actium of 31 BC pictured here including the intrigue surrounding Mark Antony, Cleopatra VII, and Octavian (Augustus Caesar). Rome was already well established in the region, so there is no change in kingship. This battle is also the ending of the Roman civil war and rival feud of consuls inside the

4) The word "time" is used in verse 24 and some to see this as a prophetic time period of 360 years. The Battle of Actium occurred in 31 BC and if 360 years are added, we come to AD 330, which is the date Constantine moved the Roman capital to Constantinople. However, the word for *time* here is not used to denote prophetic time. The Hebrew word `eth from Strong's H6256 means "time, especially (adverb with preposition) now, when, etc.:— after, (al-)ways, × certain, continually, evening, long, (due) season, so (long) as, (even-, evening-, noon-) tide, (meal-), what time, when."[12] No place is this word used to denote prophetic time of 360 years. Instead, the word *mow`ed* is used as from Strong's H4150 to denote a 360-year prophetic period as in "times, time and half a time" from Daniel 12:7. Hence, here in verse 24, the term simply means the period of time that God will allow this power to go on.

For these reasons, a fresh, new interpretive view of verses 23–29 is warranted.

Prophecies Regarding Rome in Daniel 2, 7, and 8

Previously we saw that Daniel 2 and 7 give overall characteristics of each kingdom. The description of the fourth beast is lengthy, but the interpretation is brief. We read in Daniel 7:17–18, "These four great beasts are four kings who shall arise out of the earth. But the saints of the Most High shall receive the kingdom and possess the kingdom forever, forever and ever." Here we see the angel is extremely short on the interpretation of four empires as if to simply say nonchalantly, "and they came to pass." The angel appears to have wanted Daniel's focus to be on the judgment and the eternal kingdom. Yet, Daniel is astounded by the fourth beast obviously because his people will be going through this time, and he has to specifically ask the angel about it.

Daniel's prophecy in chapter 8 gives another short description of the fourth beast. We read there in verses 9–10a, "Out of one of them came a little horn, which grew exceedingly great toward the south, toward the east, and toward the glorious land. It grew great…" This is essentially one verse to describe the worst, most devastating beast, longest-lasting beast power from ch 2 and 7. In Daniel 8:9–10, the horizontal movement of the

---

12 H6256—`eth—Strong's Hebrew Lexicon (KJV), *Blue Letter Bible,* n.d. Retrieved September 27, 2020, from https://1ref.us/1cz.

Little Horn is short taking Asia Minor and Syria to the east, Egypt to the south, and Palestine. Then after conquering the known world, this Little Horn moves vertically to heaven. What are the important elements in the prophecy of 8–9? A ram, a goat, the sanctuary, and a boldface king tearing down the sanctuary. It seems that the angel makes almost every other element of this prophecy of more importance than this horizontal horn.

So, if the proposition presented here is correct, Imperial Rome only constitutes three verses, 20–22, in Daniel 11. How could this be the case of the most shocking and destructive of all the kingdoms Daniel has seen?

1) At Jesus' crucifixion, Satan was defeated, and a new power/kingdom began to rise. In Daniel 10:13, Michael/Jesus has to fight the king of Persia conceivably to get the decrees for the exiles to return to Jerusalem passed. We know Satan is the power behind the King of Persia resisting Michael. It would follow that any power, whether the King of the North or King of the South, who resists Michael/Jesus has Satan as their true ruler. So, when we see the Jewish Sanhedrin allying with the King of the North, the Roman Governor Pilate, to place a death sentence on the Prince of the Covenant in AD 31, we not only have an attack by the King of the North, we additionally have a church and state union with Satan as the power. However, three days later, Jesus leaves the tomb and lives defeating the King of the North with its church and state union. Now a new and different King of the North is ready to come on the scene.

2) Both Paul and John state the "Lawless One" and "Antichrist" power was at work during their day.

   2 Thessalonians 2:7–10:

   > For the mystery of lawlessness is **already at work**. Only he who now restrains it will do so until he is out of the way. And then the lawless one will be revealed, whom the Lord Jesus will kill with the breath of his mouth and bring to nothing by the appearance of his coming. **The coming of the lawless one is by the activity of Satan with all power and false signs and wonders**, and with all wicked deception for those who are perishing, because they refused to love the truth and so be saved.

1 John 4:3:

> and every spirit that does not confess Jesus is not from God. This is the spirit of the **antichrist, which you heard was coming and now is in the world already.**

3) As noted earlier, Daniel 10–12 is tied to Daniel 8 and 9 where we see time prophecies of 70 weeks and 2300 days. Our start date for both is the Decree of Artaxerxes of 457 BC with end dates of AD 34—where the prince of the covenant is cut off in crucifixion—and 1844—where Jesus begins His work in the Most Holy Place in the heavenly sanctuary. If we apply the dates from the prophecy of 8 and 9 to Daniel 11, we know that the Prince of the Covenant was cut off in verse 22 in the year AD 31 with the week of Daniel 9 ending in AD 34. The portion of Daniel's prophecy of chapter 9 ending in AD 34 with the stoning of Stephen was closed. Daniel now embarks on the remaining time prophecies not only of the 2300 but also the 1260 and 1290. Note the references to time in verses 24 to 40: "but only for a time" in verse 24, "for the end is yet to be at the time appointed" in verse 27, "At the time appointed" in verse 29, "until the time of the end, for it still awaits the appointed time" in verse 35, "till the indignation is accomplished; for what is decreed shall be done" in verse 36, and finally, "At the time of the end," in verse 40. Except for the time reference in verse 29, we have five references pointing forward towards the culmination of the 1260, 1290, and 2300-year time prophecies. Thus, using Daniel 8 and 9 as a parallel, we have transitions between verses 22 and 23 from Imperial Rome to Papal Rome in the medieval divided kingdoms and again in verses 39 and 40 from Papal Rome in the medieval divided kingdoms to Papal Rome in the end-time divided kingdoms.

4) Finally, Rome ends where its parallel passage ends. Both parallel texts end with death sentences, one on Jesus, Prince of the Covenant, and the other on Jesus' people, the People of the Covenant, or those of us in these last days.

"Armies shall be utterly swept away before him and broken, even the prince of the covenant (Jesus)."[13]

---

13 Dan. 8:22.

"And he shall pitch his palatial tents between the sea and the glorious holy mountain (Jesus' people). Yet he shall come to his end, with none to help him."[14]

The interpretation of Imperial Rome transitioning to Papal Rome in the divided kingdoms is not unprecedented. Dr. Roy Gane, Professor of Hebrew Bible and Ancient Near Eastern Languages at Andrews University, agrees with this transition. Writing in the *Journal of the Adventist Theological Society*, Gane said:

> [E]ach of the transitional verses—vv. 20–21—begins with the notice that a new protagonist arises "in his place," which indicates in this context that someone takes over the functional position, status, or office of another through a transition that is not dynastic succession. The same power under whom Christ dies in v. 22 is introduced in v. 21, which indicates that v. 21 concerns the rise of imperial Rome…Imperial Rome maintained continuity in the sense that it was also Roman, but it was a very different system of rule. So, the transition from the republic to the empire certainly was not equivalent to a dynastic succession.
>
> …Imperial Rome also took the territory of the Seleucid "king of the north," so there were no distinct kings of the north or south during this Roman period. However, the kings of the north and south reappear, beginning in v. 25. Here the king of the north is the head of the Roman church introduced in vv. 23–24 and continuing through v. 45. So, whoever the "king of the south" may be in vv. 25–30 and 40–43, he represents a major enemy of the church of Rome who functions during the same long period.[15]

For the reasons stated above, Imperial Rome begins in verse 20 and ends with the crucifixion of Jesus on Golgotha. The Papacy in the divided kingdoms begins its rise to domination in verse 23, but before we look at that let us focus on the specific interpretation of Imperial Rome in verses 20–22, verse by verse.

---

14   Dan. 9:45.
15   Roy Gane, "Methodology for the Interpretation of Daniel 11:2–12:3," *Journal of the Adventist Theological Society* 27, no. 1 (2016): 317–319. Retrieved October 29, 2020, from https://1ref.us/1d0.

Chapter 6:

Interpretation of Verses 20–22

20 "Then shall arise in his place one who shall send an exactor of tribute for the glory of the kingdom. But within a few days he shall be broken, neither in anger nor in battle."

Parallel text: 40 At the time of the end, the king of the south shall attack him, but the king of the north shall rush upon him like a whirlwind, with chariots and horsemen, and with many ships. And he shall come into countries and shall overflow and pass through.

For almost 100 years before Caesar Augustus came to power, the Roman Republic seemed to be in an endless upheaval. With new peace and prosperity reigning in the new Roman Empire, all this changed. The victor of the Roman civil wars over rivals Pompey, Julius Caesar, and Mark Antony was Octavian, who took the name of Augustus Caesar. Augustus was next King of the North to "arise in his place." He did not immediately proclaim himself emperor but instead began taking on many titles, which gave him all the powers of an emperor without having to be officially granted the title, including:

- Proconsular – authority over the Western half of the empire and general of 70 percent of the Roman legions
- Augustus - religious authority
- Princeps - first-citizen or first-leader
- Civic Crown of laurel and oak – Worn on the head of Roman generals during the Roman Triumph parades
- Consular Imperium - the power of a tribune in the Senate to include convening the Senate and people at any time, putting

forth business he wanted and being the first speaker, vetoing actions, and presiding over elections
- Imperium Proconsulare Maius, or imperium over all the proconsuls where he had the right to interfere in any province and override the decisions of any governor
- Pontifex Maximus - the high priest and administrator of the advisory or administrative of the pontifices, the most crucial position in Roman religion

Augustus instituted a tax and census system reform throughout the empire to make it more efficient. Tax farming had been the means for collecting taxes in the Roman Republic. The "farmer" pays the governor or satrap a fixed amount for the right to collect taxes in a specific region. In return, the farmer kept any profit but could take a loss if he did not collect enough taxes. Levi Matthew and Zacchaeus were part of this new Roman IRS, as noted in the last chapter. We read these words in Luke 2:1, "In those days a decree went out from Caesar Augustus that all the world should be registered." Here we have a direct link from Daniel 11 to Jesus.

On August 19, AD 14, near Naples, Italy, Caesar Augustus died after some months of declining health neither in "anger nor in battle."

21 "In his place shall arise a contemptible person to whom royal majesty has not been given. He shall come in without warning and obtain the kingdom by flatteries."

Parallel text: 41 He shall come into the glorious land. And tens of thousands shall fall, but these shall be delivered out of his hand: Edom and Moab and the main part of the Ammonites.

While Emperor Augustus Caesar was in power at the birth of Jesus, his adopted son, Tiberius Caesar, was in power at the time of Jesus' crucifixion 33 years later. Though a great military commander, he spurned court life and politics. Augustus attempted to groom his nephew, then a grandson, and still another adopted son for the throne. Each died before Augustus, leaving only Tiberius, the bottom of the barrel, left for the throne. In AD 14, when Augustus died, and the Senate did indeed proclaim him Emperor of Rome.

Secular historians say Tiberius was initially a good ruler, but after the poisoning of his son in AD 23, he soon fell out of favor with the people.

He became eccentric, aloof, and reclusive. He would leave the city to ruthless leaders who abused the people while he went off to the paradise island of Capri and committed numerous sexual debaucheries. Tiberius dies a lonely, old man in AD 37.

22 "Armies shall be utterly swept away before him and broken, even the prince of the covenant."

Parallel text: 42–45 He shall stretch out his hand against the countries, and the land of Egypt shall not escape. He shall become ruler of the treasures of gold and of silver, and all the precious things of Egypt, and the Libyans and the Cushites shall follow in his train. But news from the east and the north shall alarm him, and he shall go out with great fury to destroy and devote many to destruction. And he shall pitch his palatial tents between the sea and the glorious holy mountain. Yet he shall come to his end, with none to help him.

We can rephrase this sentence to make two complete and diverse statements:

- First, we have a political statement: "Armies shall be broken and utterly swept away before him (or the Roman army)."
- Then, we have a religious statement: "The Prince of the Covenant shall be broken and utterly swept away before him (or Rome)."

This text is unquestionably about the power of Rome, through its crushing legions, not only devoured nations around them, but was, more importantly, the power who through Pilate issued a death decree and carried it out on Jesus, the Prince of the Covenant. The Gospel of Salvation was spread like wildfire to all the nations of the world within the first few centuries just like the Three Angel's Messages will spread to all the world at the end of time.

> *The Gospel of Salvation was spread like wildfire to all the nations of the world within the first few centuries just like the Three Angel's Messages will spread to all the world at the end of time.*

Chapter 7:
Medieval Divided Kingdoms in Verses 23–39

Parallel Prophecies

We find the description and characteristics of the Medieval Divided Kingdoms in the previous prophecies.
- Daniel 2—Divided church-state power in verses 33b, 41–43
  "…its feet partly of iron and partly of clay."

  "And as you saw the feet and toes, partly of potter's clay and partly of iron, it shall be a divided kingdom, but some of the firmness of iron shall be in it, just as you saw iron mixed with the soft clay. And as the toes of the feet were partly iron and partly clay, so the kingdom shall be partly strong and partly brittle. As you saw the iron mixed with soft clay, so they will mix with one another in marriage, but they will not hold together, just as iron does not mix with clay."

- Daniel 7—Comes up among the 10 horns in verses 8, 20–21, 24–25
  "I considered the horns, and behold, there came up among them another horn, a little one, before which three of the first horns were plucked up by the roots. And behold, in this horn were eyes like the eyes of a man, and a mouth speaking great things."

  "and about the ten horns that were on its head, and the other horn that came up and before which three of them fell, the horn that had eyes and a mouth that spoke great things, and that seemed greater than its companions. As I looked, this horn made war with the saints and prevailed over them."

"He shall speak words against the Most High, and shall wear out the saints of the Most High, and shall think to change the times and the law; and they shall be given into his hand for a time, times, and half a time."

- Daniel 8—Attacks the Daily Sanctuary Practices in verses 10–14, 23–25
"It grew great, even to the host of heaven. And some of the host and some of the stars it threw down to the ground and trampled on them. It became great, even as great as the Prince of the host. And the regular burnt offering was taken away from him, and the place of his sanctuary was overthrown. And a host will be given over to it together with the regular burnt offering because of transgression, and it will throw truth to the ground, and it will act and prosper. Then I heard a holy one speaking, and another holy one said to the one who spoke, 'For how long is the vision concerning the regular burnt offering, the transgression that makes desolate, and the giving over of the sanctuary and host to be trampled underfoot?' And he said to me, 'For 2,300 evenings and mornings. Then the sanctuary shall be restored to its rightful state.'"

"And at the latter end of their kingdom, when the transgressors have reached their limit, a king of bold face, one who understands riddles, shall arise. His power shall be great—but not by his own power; and he shall cause fearful destruction and shall succeed in what he does, and destroy mighty men and the people who are the saints. By his cunning he shall make deceit prosper under his hand, and in his own mind he shall become great. Without warning he shall destroy many. And he shall even rise up against the Prince of princes, and he shall be broken—but by no human hand."

- Daniel 9—Abomination of Desolation in verse 27c
"And on the wing of abominations shall come one who makes desolate, until the decreed end is poured out on the desolator."

The Focus of Daniel 11: 23–39

The above verses would indicate that Daniel 11: 23–39 must center around 1) the establishment of a church-state system, 2) in Western Europe, and 3) which makes decrees and laws replacing the covenant and the sanctuary ministry. Daniel 10–12 is also about God's People. While there are numerous significant events during this period, only the events directly linking the above elements would presumably be included in verses 23–39. The events build on one another into a crescendo just before 1798 to create one head of a church-state system in Europe who pretends to be God on earth and has replaced all the "continual" sanctuary ministries including changing the ten commandments. All this directly impact God's Covenant keeping people who are detested, separated, and persecuted by the church-state systems.

The above verses would indicate that Daniel 11: 23–39 must center around 1) the establishment of a church-state system, 2) in Western Europe, and 3) which makes decrees and laws replacing the covenant and the sanctuary ministry.

The Missing Element in Daniel's Time Prophecies

Each of Daniel's time prophecies "[t]ime, times, and ½ a times" (Daniel 7), 2300 Days (Daniel 8), and 70 Weeks (Daniel 9) have corresponding prophetic event narratives, which are, then, matched to a literal historical event. However, neither Daniel 2, 7, or 8 and 9 give a corresponding prophetic event for the 1290 days and 1335 days.

Time Prophecy	Corresponding Event Prophecy	Literal Historical Event
"Time, times, and ½ a times" Daniel 7 and 12	Daniel 7:24 "As for the ten horns, out of this kingdom ten kings shall arise, and another shall arise after them" Daniel 7:26 "But the court shall sit in judgment, and his dominion shall be taken away, to be consumed and destroyed to the end."	This began in 538 when the Papacy had all three elements to rule Christendom: a temporal power arm (508 Frankish kingdom), authority (533 the letter from the Emperor), and domination to operate from (538 the defeat of the Ostrogoths from Rome). It ended in 1798 when the French Directory ordered General Berthier to capture and exile the pope removing his temporal authority.
2300 Days Daniel 8	Daniel 8:14, "And he said to me, "For 2,300 evenings and mornings. Then the sanctuary shall be restored to its rightful state."	This is the heavenly Day of Atonement which began 2,300 years from the Decree of Artaxerxes in 457 BC. In 1844, Jesus, our High Priest, entered the Most Holy Place in Heaven.

Time Prophecy	Corresponding Event Prophecy	Literal Historical Event
70 Weeks Daniel 9	Daniel 9:24, "Seventy weeks are decreed about your people and your holy city, to finish the transgression, to put an end to sin, and to atone for iniquity, to bring in everlasting righteousness, to seal both vision and prophet, and to anoint a most holy place.	Our starting point is the same as the 2300 Days with the decree Artaxerxes decree in 457 BC. Jesus started His earthly ministry in week 70, which was AD 27 at His baptism. In the middle of the week, AD 31, He was crucified and ended the sacrificial service. Then in AD 34, at the end of the week, after Stephan's defense before the Jewish Sanhedrin, he was stoned and the 70-week probationary period for the Jews closed.
1290 Days Daniel 12	?	We know this time period links with Daniel 7 and the time, times, and half a time which ended in 1798, so if we move back 1290 year, we come to 508.
1335 Days Daniel 12	?	We know this period links with Daniel 8 and the 2300 days, which ended in 1844. Notice the phrasing of Daniel 12:12, "Blessed is he who waits and arrives at the 1,335 days." Obviously, those who lived after October 22, 1844, did not consider themselves blessed. However, those same people certainly felt blessed and euphoric for the year prior to that date; and indeed, they were blessed. Hence, 1843–1335 leads us back to the year 508.

If these prophetic days of 1290 and 1335 began in 508, the corresponding prophetic events must be found in the prophecy in Daniel 11.

Previously in Daniel 7, we saw a time prophecy with *time, times and half a time*, and then, in Daniel 8 we see 2300 days. These prophecies started in AD 538 and 457 BC and ended in 1798 and 1844, respectively. Revelation 10:6 makes known that these will be the last time-setting prophecies.

Let us consider the 1290 time period dealing with Papal Rome's temporal power. If we take 1798 and subtract 1290, we get 508, but in Daniel 7, the start day was 538. So, we have two start dates and one end date for the rise and end of the Papal Church-State system.

Just like we saw Greece's power rising while there was still a Medo-Persian king remaining, the Greek Hellenistic Kingdoms continued as the Roman power rose. Likewise, the church-state kingdom began rising while the Roman empire was in decline until the ten horn kingdoms of chapter 7 finally overran Imperial Rome. Now, if we look back at our parallel prophecy on Greece, we see one start date and two fall dates. Greece had one fixed start date of 331 BC when Alexander defeated the Persians at the Battle of Gaugamela but had a gradual decline starting in 188 BC with the Treaty of Apamea and ultimately ending the kingdom in 31 BC at the Battle of Actium.

Juxtapose this with Papal Rome's gradual rise in 508 and with the baptism of Clovis I, giving the Papacy the army of power, in 533 when Emperor Justin gave Pope John III authority over the former Western Roman Empire,[16] and the full force of that union in 538 when the Ostrogoths were driven from Rome by General Belisarius as explained in *Ministry Magazine*, "Why the Year 538?"[17] Papal Rome had full ecclesiastical control over the region of the former Western Roman Empire which included a temporal power to accomplish its dogmas. Now, we come to one fixed date for the end of Papal Rome when in 1798 the Revolutionary French Directory orders General Berthier to invade Rome and to capture and exile Pope Pius VI. We see an apparent reversal of the process from previous kingdoms having one fixed start date with a gradual fall between where the next power arises and the complete collapse of the kingdom. With Papal Rome, we see the opposite with a gradual rise with a fixed fall date.

Kingdom	Start Date	End Date
Greece	**331 BC**	188 BC Treaty of Apamea 168 BC Battle of Pydna 65 BC Greek Mithridates Rebellion 31 BC Battle of Actium
Medieval Divided Kingdoms	AD 476 End of the Western Empire AD 508 Clovis' Baptism AD 533 Justin's Letter to Pope AD 538 Ostrogoths defeated at Rome	**AD 1798**

---

16 Thomas William Allies, "Justinian," *The Formation of Christendom* VI, n.d. Retrieved September 27, 2020, from https://1ref.us/1d2.

17 C. Bollman, "Why the Year 538?" *Ministry Magazine*, 1931. Retrieved September 27, 2020, from https://1ref.us/1d3.

As to the 1335 days dealing with Papal Rome's trampling down of the sanctuary services, if we start at AD 508 and add 1335 years, we get 1843. YLT states, "O the blessedness of him who is waiting earnestly, and doth come to the days, a thousand, three hundred, thirty and five."[18] Certainly, October 23, 1844, was the most bitter, disappointing day ever, but the previous year was the sweetest time to have lived because they were sure Jesus was coming the following year. In this disappointment, we have another parallel. God's people experienced exuberance and excitement in 1843 and 1844; likewise, the Jews experienced the same emotions at Jesus' triumphal entry into Jerusalem. Both of these events were followed by disappointment, bewilderment, and hopelessness when Christ did not return and when He hung up on the cross of Golgotha, respectively.

---

18   Dan. 12:12.

Chapter 8:
Historical Context of Daniel 11:23–39

While studying Daniel 11 verses 23–31 in the *SDA Bible Commentary*, the fact that verse 22 leads us to the crucifixion in AD 31 struck me, but the remaining verses in this section doubled back to 161 BC and this alliance between the Jews and the Roman Republic, a backtrack of 192 years! At no previous time has Daniel doubled back in his prophecies. The line is always progressive. Christian M. Sorenson at the 1919 Seventh-day Adventist Bible Conference also took issue with interpretations that double back over time: "[P]rophecy runs in a successive line from the time it was uttered to the coming of Christ. That is the ordinary way of interpreting prophecy." The 1919 Bible Conference was debating a "view that would introduce Rome as early as the 14th verse," then return to the Seleucid kings, to Rome as the crucifiers of Prince of the covenant in AD 31, and then back to the Battle of Actium in 31 BC. He continues, "I should call in railroad terms a 'switchback'—where the line runs on a certain distance, and then turns back. [There] is a law of prophetic interpretations when a line of historic consecutive prophecy is connected and goes in on a straight line. In this case, there is a 'switchback'"[19] in prophetic time.

Many, including C.M. Sorenson, have attempted to interpret Daniel on a purely chronological line of prophecy. None have passed the test of time nor have the majority of Adventist scholars accepted them. Yet, not a few Adventist scholars have voiced their uncomfortableness of the predominant "switchback" interpretations of Daniel 11. So, why a new position now? I can only reply: "For such a time as this." As seen over and over in Scripture and the history of our church, God at times reveals

---

19   C. Sorenson, Seventh-day Adventist Bible Conference, 1919. Retrieved October 29, 2020, from https://1ref.us/1d4.

truth progressively, a little here a little there, or He waits for the precise moment it is needed. I believe, based on current world conditions, including the attacks on the separation of church and state, the rebirth of the prominence and power of the Papacy, and the loss of individual freedom of conscience, the time must be now.

Even so, let us move on now to this new interpretation of verses 23–29. Based on previous prophecies in Daniel, we know it is a divided church-state power, which comes up among the 10 horns in Europe, and it will attack the daily sanctuary practices, set up the abomination of desolation, and change the commandments. Below, these elements are divided out, but quite often, they overlap.

Church-State Systems

There are significant parallels between the breakup of the Greek kingdoms and the church-state systems of the medieval divided kingdoms. To begin, Alexander had five generals, but by 301 BC at the Battle of Ipsus, only four generals remained to divide the kingdom of Alexander. At the Council of Constantinople in AD 381, only four Bishoprics retained power[20] after the breakup of the Imperial Roman Empire.

Greece and Medieval Divided Kingdoms Parallel Rulers

Kings of Greece	Kings of Church-State Systems
KON Seleucus ended 168 BC	KON Rome ended 1798
KOS Ptolemy ended 188 BC	KOS Constantinople ended 1453
Lysimachus ended 281 BC	Alexandria ended 641
Cassander ended 294 BC	Antioch ended 637
Antigonus I in 301 BC	Jerusalem ended 637

In the Greek kingdom breakup, Ptolemy of Egypt in the south came up first to control the Glorious Land. Likewise, the Bishop of Constantinople where the emperor resided controlled the Christian church as "the seat of the New Rome." Most Adventist scholars believe Imperial Rome became the King of the North after Seleucia was defeated at the Battle of Pydna in 168 BC. If Papal Rome grew out of Imperial Rome as the King of the North, it would stand to reason that the King of the South would be a power creating a "great conflict" (Daniel 10:1) with Papal Rome. History describes a great struggle for authority with the Roman Emperor in Constantinople and the Bishop of the East. Moreover, Constantinople

---

20 "First Council of Constantinople," Wikipedia, The Free Encyclopedia, 2020. Retrieved September 29, 2020, from https://1ref.us/1d5.

is southeast of Rome, and the Byzantine empire included regions south of Rome such as Egypt, west Africa, Sicily, and the southern section of the Italian peninsula. By AD 508, the region of the King of the North greatly expanded with the conversion of the Frankish peoples.

***Byzantine Empire AD 527*[21]**

Additionally, like the Roman Republic was a power on the rise confronting both the Ptolemys and the Seleucids, Islam was a power on the rise confronting both Rome and Constantinople, which eventually captured the latter. Furthermore, Islam had engulfed the three Bishoprics east of Constantinople of Alexandria, Jerusalem, and Antioch by AD 641. While Imperial Rome conquered the Greek King of the North, Seleucia, Islam would not conquer Papal Rome, as the King of the North, because the prophecy of Daniel 8:11 states that Papal Rome would extend until the second coming.

As long as the capital of the Roman Empire was in Rome, the Bishop of Rome was the head of all the Bishoprics. When Constantine moved the capital to Constantinople in AD 330, this changed dramatically. As the "New Rome," the secular protection and ecclesiastical authority migrated from Rome to Constantinople. This move left Rome literally out on a limb of the empire. The popes immediately went to work in regaining their position at the top of the universal Christian church. This led to tensions not only with the other Bishoprics but with the emperor, who was the official head of the Christian church. With the Bishoprics of Antioch and Alexandria waning in power, the Bishopric of Constantinople worked hand in hand with the emperor. Rome, on the other hand, was surrounded by Barbarian nations and most probably felt she must exert her authority

---

21   Map retrieved October 29, 2020, from https://1ref.us/1d6.

in church ecclesiastical matters over the other Bishoprics. An example of this tension with the Bishoprics was seen in 445. Pope Leo disputed with Patriarch Dioscorus of Alexandria insisting that the ecclesiastical practice of Alexandria be under his authority and control. He reasoned Peter was the Bishop of Rome and the highest authority in the church. Mark the Evangelist, Peter's subordinate, established the church in Alexandria. Therefore, the Bishop of Rome, or the Papacy, was superior to the Bishop of Alexandria and all other bishoprics.

The tensions between Rome and Constantinople resulted in the power struggle of the Great East-West Schism.[22] Controversial issues included the Iconoclast controversy (the veneration of images), the use of unleavened versus leavened bread in the Mass, celibacy of the clergy, and the filioque. This last factor continues to be the main point of disagreement even until today. The First Council of Nicaea in 325 produced the Nicaean Creed—a statement of belief used in Christian worship. The issue: the West added the phrase "and the son," or the filioque. Where the church in Rome wanted the creed to say, "The Holy Spirit proceeds from the Father and the Son" the Eastern church opposed this and wanted the creed to only say, "The Holy Spirit proceeds from the Father."

One of the lowest points for Rome in the struggle for supremacy in the church was during the Three Chapters incident resulting after the Second Council of Constantinople in 553. Pope Vigilius refused to attend and issued a document forbidding the Council. When he would not consent to the Council's main edict—the condemnation of the so-called Three Chapters—the emperor held him captive in Constantinople for eight years.[23]

For many years the schism amounted to a war of words and edicts as seen in 858 when Emperor Michael III deposed the Patriarch of Constantinople. Because Pope Nicholas I believed he alone had the right of deposition, the pope deposed the emperor and reinstated the former Patriarch.[24] Hence, the emperor deposed the pope.

The schism got bloody with the Massacre of the Latins in 1182. Catholics, or Latins, were murdered or forced to flee out of Constantinople. Later, in 1202 Pope Innocent III called for the Fourth Crusade, but things went awry, and the crusaders ended up sacking Constantinople in 1204, putting the emperor and the church clergy to flight and occupying the city for some years afterward.

---

22 "East–West Schism," Wikipedia, The Free Encyclopedia, September 28, 2020. Retrieved September 29, 2020, from https://1ref.us/1d7.
23 "Pope Vigilius," February 22, 2019. Retrieved September 27, 2020, from https://1ref.us/1d8.
24 "Pope Nicholas I," Wikipedia, The Free Encyclopedia, September 16, 2020. Retrieved September 29, 2020, from https://1ref.us/1d9.

Finally, in 1453 the Ottoman Empire captured Constantinople partly because the Byzantine Empire never fully recovered from the sack of the Latins. With the fall of Constantinople, Rome was the last Bishopric standing to retain open ecclesiastical authority and temporal power over Europe and the Catholic colonies around the world.

While Protestant nations began breaking away from the control of Rome in the Middle Ages, many set up church-state systems of their own just as oppressive in England, Switzerland, Germany, and others. Church-state systems still dominate many nations in Europe and around the world today, though most currently extend religious freedom to those who are not of the official church. Yet, we know and can see ample signs, that tolerance of individual conscience in religious matters will come to a swift end.

Europe

Political division in Europe, North Africa and Near East after the end of the Western Roman Empire in 476 AD[25]

King Odoacer of Italy

While the exact Germanic descent of Flavius Odoacer is debated, he was a Barbarian soldier in the Roman Army who deposed the child

---
25   Map retrieved October 29, 2020, from https://1ref.us/1da.

emperor Romulus Augustulus and became King of Italy from 476–493. During his reign, Odoacer was on good relations with Pope Felix III, although he remained an Arian Christian—a reason for contention with the Byzantine Empire.

Three Uprooted Horns

- The Heruli settled on the Danube River around 500 under King Rodulph. However, by 508, he lost his entire kingdom to the Lombards.
- The Vandals came down through Gaul and Spain and settled in North Africa, Sicily, and Corsica. Emperor Justinian wanted to reclaim the western portion of the empire and exterminate Arianism. In 534, General Belisarius defeated the remnants of the Vandal kingdom and expelled them from the Byzantine Empire.
- The Ostrogoths were also Arian and settled on the Italian Peninsula after defeating and killing Odoacer in 493. Theodoric the Great reigned from 454 to 526 and kept good relations with the Papacy. The period from 493 to 537 is known as the Ostrogothic Papacy where the Arian Ostrogoths had in large part determined who would be Pope. In 535, after defeating the Vandals in Africa, Belisarius continued the war onto the Italian peninsula against the Ostrogoths in Justinian's effort to root out Arianism. In 537, Belisarius reached Rome and occupied it. It was soon besieged by an overwhelming number of Goths under their King Vitiges. After a series of battles and with both sides suffering from disease and famine, Belisarius defeated over half of the Gothic force at the infamous Milvian Bridge, sending the rest of the Goths to flight and ending the siege in 538. It is at this point that the Papacy was able to occupy Rome under Christian rule, and the *time, times, and half a time* (1260 years) of the prophecy of Daniel 7:25 began.

However, in 552, the new Ostrogothic King Totila led a resistance against the Byzantines. General Narses soundly defeated the Ostrogoths, after which they lost their autonomy, ethnic identity, and merged with the Lombards. Even so, it is clear that the Arian Ostrogoth's found defeat at Rome in 538, and this began the 1260 year prophecy as is explained in *Ministry Magazine*, "[I]t was the beginning of its downfall, and so opened the way for the development of the Papacy not possible as long as Italy, if not Rome itself, was governed by an Arian power, or indeed by any ruler whose authority was primarily civil."[26]

---
26   C. Bollman, "Year 538."

Seven Remaining Horns

- The Alemanni settled in the region of Switzerland. However, Clovis I defeated them in 496 at the Battle of Tolbiac, absorbed them into the Frankish kingdom, and they became Catholics.
- The Anglo-Saxons had settled in the region of Great Britain by 450. Pope Gregory I in 595 sent Augustine to Britain, and he began converting the Anglo-Saxons. In 664, the Church of England at the Synod of Whitby declared its allegiance to the Pope. Augustine was the first Archbishop of Canterbury.
- The Suevi had settled in the region of Portugal around 410. Arianism was soon introduced and continued until around 550 when they began practicing the Catholic-Orthodox faith.
- The Visigoths moved into the Roman Empire beginning in 376 and defeated the Romans at the Battle of Adrianople in 378. Under Alaric I, they invaded Italy and sacked Rome in 410. They settled in southern Gaul, but in 507, they were defeated by the Franks under Clovis I at the Battle of Vouillé. From there, they moved into the region of Spain. While the Visigoths became Arians, in 587, the Visigoth King Reccared I converted and began a slow process of transitioning from Arianism to Catholicism.
- The Burgundians settled in the region of Southern France. Clotilde, a Burgundian princess and Catholic, married Clovis I, but war broke out in 500, and King Gundobad was forced to give the Franks an annual tribute. However, in 532 at the Battle of Autun, the Franks defeated and absorbed the Burgundian kingdom.
- The Bavarians settled in the region of Southern Germany on the Danube River. Catholicism to the populous grew slowly in Bavaria through its Catholic dukes. In 724, Pope Gregory II sent Bishop Corbinian to evangelize the region. Earlier, in 716, Bavaria became part of the Frankish Carolingians Dynasty and was absorbed into the Holy Roman Empire.
- The Franks were Germanic tribes that migrated down from the Lower Rhine and the Ems Rivers into Northwest Gaul. Starting in 428, under King Childeric I and his son Clovis I, the Merovingian family began to dominate the other Frankish peoples.

Frankish Kingdom

Because of its magnitude presence in Church history, this kingdom needs more than a simple bullet point. Clovis I united the Frankish kingdom, baptized into Catholicism, and ushered in Catholicism as the state religion over Arianism and pagan practices. However, the Franks were different from other kingdoms around them. Instead of just having a state religion, they exported Catholicism and forced conversions of all the peoples they conquered. Early on, this became the military arm of the Papacy beginning in 508 when Emperor Anastasius I Dicorus gives Clovis a Roman consulship. The following year, Clovis captured and executed a former ally, Ragnachar, king of Cambrai, and his brother, Ricchar, who would not accept Clovis's conversion from paganism to Catholicism and were actively recruiting defecting pagans to their side against Clovis. Even so, the later kings grew weak and did not expand "Christendom" much further. It was the year 508 that the 1290 years, the 1335 years of Daniel 12:11–12, and the abomination of desolation of the Church-State persecuting power began. It should be, similarly, noted that at the start of the 1290-year period, King Clovis at the basilica of Saint Martin in Tours, France, in the presence of Catholic Bishop Remigius, crowned himself king of Franks.[27] At the end of that period in 1804, Napoleon at the Notre-Dame Cathedral in Paris, France, took the crown from Pope Pius VII and likewise crowned himself Emperor.

In 732, the military leader and Prince of the Palace, Charles Martel, of the Carolingian family, defeated the Muslims in the Battle of Tours. However, he refused Pope Gregory III's offer to the title of Roman Consulship and defender of the Holy See, and he also declined the Pope's plea to come to his aid against the Lombards, a longtime ally of the Franks.

While Charles declined the Papal invites, one of his sons, Pepin the Short (or the Younger), conspired with Pope Zachary to depose the last Merovingian king and proclaimed himself king. Pepin not only expanded his temporal power but that of the churches also. At the bidding of Pope Stephan II, he defeated the Lombards, who were harassing Rome and the church in Italy. After their defeat, Pepin gave the land to the pope. This is known as The Donation of Pepin which became the Papal States. The pope now not only had a wide influence over Europe, but he was also the legal head of his own nation-state.

Pepin's son, Charlemagne, expanded the Frankish empire even more, and in 800 the pope crowned him as Emperor of the Holy Roman Empire. From this point forward, the Papacy had ecclesiastical authority over all Western Europe, a military arm in the Kingdom of the Franks and the

---

27 R. Mathisen, "Clovis, Anastasius, and Political Status in 508 C.E.: The Frankish Aftermath of the Battle of Vouille," in *The Battle of Vouillé, 507 CE: Where France Began* (Berlin/Boston: De Gruyter, 2012), 106. Retrieved October 29, 2020, from https://1ref.us/1db.

Holy Roman Empire, and was now a sovereign state of their own, subject to no one.

Wildcard Kingdom

The Lombards, a Germanic tribe, descended from a small tribe called the Winnili, originally from southern Scandinavia before migrating to the region of Austria and Slovakia north of the Danube River. The Gothic War between the Byzantines and the Ostrogoths ravished the Italian peninsula. By 572, well after the fall of the Western Roman Empire, they had established the Lombard Kingdom in north and central Italy. In 592, the Lombards were at the gates of Rome, Pope Gregory I negotiated with the Lombards and agreed to pay an annual tribute, and they withdrew. The Lombards would control the area around Rome, often harassing the residents of the city and the church until 774, when Charlemagne conquered their kingdom at the pleading of the pope.

"Not Mix Together"

Daniel 2:43 specifically states, "they will mix with one another in marriage, but they will not hold together," and this prophecy still stands today. Many have done well researching the lines of marriages in Europe between kings and queens as seen in this prophecy. All through the Bible and the ancient world, inheritance was through primogeniture or the passing on of inheritance property and estate to the eldest son, but Europe was different. Whereas the Byzantine Empire commonly had one successor, many kings of Europe partitioned their estates between all their sons. Even if a king enlarged his region and spread Catholicism as the religion of the land, it would be redistributed between his heirs. This was the case with the Merovingian Frankish Dynasty of Clovis I and again with the Carolingian Frankish Dynasty of Charlemagne, which weakened the kingdom after each succession. One attempt for European kings to retain power in the hands of the family was to "mix with one another in marriage," but of course, this was futile because the Bible prophesied against these schemes, and in turn, these marriage alliances often had devastating results.

Consequently, unlike Constantinople, where there was only one Emperor to deal with, the popes had to repetitively maneuver and work with these kings and rulers using rewards like crownings, titles, and relics, or by threats of anathemas, ex-communication, and populace uprisings. Try as they may, they could not turn Europe into a unified and sustainable empire through bribery, wars, and intermarriages. It could not be done, and the prophecy of Daniel 2 still stands today despite the latest attempts through the European Union.

While Rome was located on the Italian peninsula, Catholicism had a difficult time rooting itself there. From the days following the transfer of the Roman capital to Constantinople, diverse Germanic tribes such as Lombards, the Sicilians, Sardinians, and Ostrogoths surrounded Rome. In the 5th century, while the Ostrogoths controlled the northern section of the peninsula, the lower portion was still part of the Byzantine Empire for many years and derived much of its doctrines and practices from Constantinople and not Rome. However, the Byzantine empire was out of the region completely by 751 when the Lombards invaded Rome and the Pope had to seek assistance from the Franks. With the defeat of the Lombards, the Franks gave the region known as the Papal States to the Pope. In return, Pope Stephen anointed Pepin the Short of the Franks and titled him Patricius Romanorum. In 800, with Pope Leo III crowning Charlemagne emperor of the Holy Roman Empire and giving him the title of Imperator Romanorum, the northern and central section of the Italian peninsula was solidly under Catholic temporal control.

Attacks on the Covenant and the Sanctuary

If a nation speaks through the laws it legislates, then it would stand that a church speaks through its doctrines and councils, and in the case of the Catholic Church, when the Pope speaks ex-cathedra. It is obvious from the progression of the councils that the churches of the East attempted to hold fast to the practices of the 1st-century church by holding on to the Sabbath, forbidding idolatry, and allowing priests to marry. However, the Church at Rome was heavily influenced by the ancient Roman pagan practices and by the pagan nations around them and slowly brought those into the church.

One of the earliest pagan changes came between the 2nd and 4th centuries involving the day of worship. The Bible records no such change from the Sabbath to Sunday, and there is good reason to believe it was not changed in the apostles' day. If circumcision created such an uproar in the early church, imagine what the uproar would have been like over changing the day of worship, but there is no change recorded in the Bible. The Apostle Paul during his trials states emphatically, "But this I confess to you, that according to the Way, which they call a sect, I worship the God of our fathers, believing everything laid down by the Law and written in the Prophets,"[28] and again, "Paul argued in his defense, 'Neither against

---
28 Acts 24:14.

the law of the Jews, nor against the temple, nor against Caesar have I committed any offense.'"[29]

We also know from early church documents that the seventh-day Sabbath was still in practice in the 2nd century. Written around AD 65–80, the Didache, or "Teaching of the Twelve Apostles," while not specifically mentioning the Sabbath, states, "fast on the fourth day and the Preparation."[30] If they were keeping Sunday in AD 80, they would not allude to the preparation day. Also, the disputed Epistle of Barnabas, written between AD 70 and 132, uses "Sabbath" eight times with no references to Sunday or the Lord's Day. In the Epistle of Barnabas 15:1, it states, "Moreover concerning the Sabbath likewise it is written in the Ten Words, in which He spake to Moses face to face on Mount Sinai; And ye shall hallow the Sabbath of the Lord with pure hands and with a pure heart." However, the writer states in Barnabas 15:9, "Wherefore also we keep the eighth day for rejoicing, in the which also Jesus rose from the dead, and having been manifested ascended into the heavens." So, we see both Sabbath-keeping and reverence for Sunday as early as AD 132.

While the change continued slowly in the 2nd century and is well documented in Adventist literature, it culminated with the decree of Emperor Constantine in AD 321:

> On the venerable Day of the Sun let the magistrates and people residing in cities rest, and let all workshops be closed. In the country, however, persons engaged in agriculture may freely and lawfully continue their pursuits; because it often happens that another day is not so suitable for grain-sowing or for vine-planting; lest by neglecting the proper moment for such operations the bounty of heaven should be lost.

Past scholars on Daniel have correctly focused on the infallibility ex-cathedra statements of the Pontiffs. Even so, much can be learned from a focus on the ecumenical councils of the Catholic Church, and this section will focus on the actions of those councils which affect the true people of God. Much of this section is taken from the online article called "The 21 Ecumenical Councils"[31] (see appendix B for the full article, which contains a summary of each council).

---

29 Acts 25:8.
30 J. Lightfoot, "Didache," 2001. Retrieved September 27, 2020, from https://1ref.us/1dc.
31 K. Keating, "The 21 Ecumenical Councils," December 5, 2019. Retrieved September 27, 2020, from https://1ref.us/1dd.

We can glean much as to the mindset of the Papacy through these councils.

- The usurpation of temporal power by the pope in Rome of the former Western Roman Empire from the Byzantine Emperor in Constantinople.
- The development and growth of papal authority.
- The progression of persecution of heretics.
- The pagan influences including veneration of image worship acceptance.
- Tradition as being equal to, then superior to Scripture.
- The development of the mass and Eucharist.

Council of Nicaea, 325 Byzantine Empire

The first official empire-wide council at Nicaea was in 325, called by Constantine the Great. It was to determine the date for Easter, not based on the Passover, but on the first Sunday after the first full moon following the vernal equinox. While technically not linked to a pagan holiday, it did establish the foundation for the authority to *"change times and laws."* The council also established a creed which listed the beliefs of the Church. While based on portions of Scripture, this creed and future adaptations would become of more importance than Scripture itself.

Council of Laodicea,[32] 364 Byzantine Empire

This council focused on the Sabbath question. Both Sabbath and Sunday were addressed in Canons 49 and 51, and the council's wording gives clear evidence that Western churches were all keeping Sunday, but the Eastern churches still regarded the seventh-day Sabbath. Additionally, it is interesting that Canon 35 forbade idolatry, which is why later councils do not use this term "idol," but instead, the council would decree the "veneration" of icons and images was permissible. The idea is that one is not praying to an idol but, simply, praying to what the image or icon represents, i.e., the Saints, Mary, or Jesus.

Council of Constantinople I, 381 Byzantine Empire

Persecution of Arians began after this council. Arians believed Jesus was only human and not divine. While we believe this is nonbiblical, we do not believe our state or federal government should criminalize Arians of today, such as the Jehovah's Witnesses or, closer to home, to some extent,

---

[32] Synod of Laodicea (4th Century), New Advent, n.d. Retrieved September 27, 2020, from https://1ref.us/1de.

the anti-trinitarian Seventh-day Adventists belief that at some point Jesus did not exist with the Father.

Council of Ephesus, 431 Byzantine Empire

While the veneration of Mary began before this time, the council codified an unbiblical belief about Mary. The council upheld the vernation of Mary as sinless, the assumption or ascendancy of Mary to heaven, the immaculate conception, and finally, Mary being Co-Redemptrix with Christ. These all would give rise to prayer to Mary. The Catholic Douay-Rhimes Bible of 1899 translates Genesis 3:15 as "*she* shall crush thy head, and thou shalt lie in wait for *her* heel."

Council of Constantinople II, 553 Byzantine Empire

While doctrinally little took place during this council, the significance lies in the display of animosity and struggle between Rome and Constantinople. This council led to the capture of the pope. The emperor only released the pope after he accepted the condemnation of the "Three Chapters." Clearly, in 553, the Byzantine emperor in Constantinople had the upper hand, but the Papacy was not going to submit for long.

Council of Nicaea II, 787 Byzantine Empire

This council was over the continued struggle to bring in idol worship—veneration of images and icons—into the church. Condemned at the council was the practice of Iconoclasm—the attack or rejection of the belief in the importance of icons and images. The council upheld the adoration of icons and images that Protestants during the Reformation would rightly consider as idolatry.

Council of Constantinople IV, 870 Byzantine Empire

Again, we have the issue of papal authority over the other bishoprics and the emperor. The pope believed the emperor had to get his approval before appointing or deposing bishops. The council, following the mandate of the pope, deposed Photius as the patriarch of Constantinople officially ending a schism between East and West, at least for a time.

Council of Lateran I, 1123 Holy Roman Empire

The controversy over church authority between the popes and emperors did not end when Rome created the Holy Roman Empire, nor when she subsequently divorced herself from the Byzantines empire. The emperor had appointed bishops in his kingdom, even though the popes said they alone should appoint bishops. This council eliminated secular leaders from appointing minor officials in the church, but they could have an unofficial but significant influence in the appointment of bishops and significant leaders.

Council of Lateran II, 1139 Holy Roman Empire

This council continued to uphold nonbiblical practices in the church, reaffirming infant baptism, the sacramental nature of the priesthood and marriage, the Eucharist, and condemning the marriage of priests. Catholic doctrine teaches that grace is merited out by the priesthood through the seven sacraments which includes baptism. The more grace merited to you by the church on earth, the less will your time be in purgatory. In the Bible, a person is justified through repentance, accepting Jesus as one's Savior, and being baptized by immersion into the death and resurrection of Jesus to a new life. In the Eucharist, the bread and wine become the actual blood and flesh of Christ, and He is re-sacrificed every time the mass is dispensed. The more masses the lay member takes part in, then the more grace is dispensed to them. Yet, the Bible is clear that Jesus was sacrificed once for all. The council also condemned all who did not believe the mass was the physical sacrificed body and blood of Jesus.

Council of Lateran III, 1179 Holy Roman Empire

The council put the Papacy in a position to persecute "heretics" using the state powers in France and the Holy Roman Empire, specifically against the Waldenses and Albigenses, against anyone who opposed the official church doctrine.

Council of Lateran IV, 1215 Holy Roman Empire

This council revisited the doctrine of the Eucharist and defining "transubstantiation" to explain the real presence of Jesus in the mass. "His body and blood are truly contained in the sacrament of the altar under the forms of bread and wine, the bread and wine having been transubstantiated, by God's power, into his body and blood. Nobody can effect this sacrament except a priest who has been properly ordained according to the church's keys, which Jesus Christ himself gave to the apostles and their successors."[33] Penance was also added as one of the seven sacraments.

Council of Lyons I, 1245 Holy Roman Empire

This council excommunicated and deposed Frederick II for heresy and crimes against the Church.

---

33 Fourth Lateran Council: 1215 Council Fathers, December 12, 2017. Retrieved September 27, 2020, from https://1ref.us/1df.

Council of Lyons II, 1274 Holy Roman Empire

The difference between East and West was put aside to plan a crusade, but it never materialized; and tensions between Rome and Constantinople continued. This council did make a definition for the doctrine of Purgatory: "Because if they die truly repentant in charity before they have made satisfaction by worthy fruits of penance for (sins) committed and omitted, their souls are cleansed after death by purgatorical or purifying punishments...and to relieve punishments of this kind, the offerings of the living faithful are of advantage to these, namely, the sacrifices of Masses, prayers, alms, and other duties of piety, which have customarily been performed by the faithful for the other faithful according to the regulations of the Church."[34]

Council of Constance, 1414 Holy Roman Empire

This council specifically opposed the teachings of John Wycliffe and John Huss for teaching sola scriptura, denying the authority of the pope and bishops, denying the real presence of Christ in the Eucharist, and writing against penance and indulgence. Wycliff, 1330 to 1384, was seen as the Morning Star of the Reformation and translated the first English Bible. Huss from Bohemia, 1369 to 1415, is recorded saying during his execution, "God is my witness that the things charged against me I never preached. In the same truth of the Gospel which I have written, taught, and preached, drawing upon the sayings and positions of the holy doctors, I am ready to die today."[35]

The Council of Florence, 1443 Holy Roman Empire

Papal supremacy over ecumenical councils had been challenged from the earliest days of the Catholic Church. This council decreed: "We likewise define that the Holy Apostolic See, and the Roman Pontiff, hold the primacy throughout the entire world; and that the Roman Pontiff himself is the successor of blessed Peter, the chief of the Apostles, and the true vicar of Christ, and that he is the head of the entire Church, and the father and teacher of all Christians; and that full power was given to him in blessed Peter by our Lord Jesus Christ, to feed, rule, and govern the universal Church."[36]

Additionally, there was a last gesture to reconcile Rome and Eastern Churches, but this was short-lived. Ultimately, the 1500-year-old Byzantine

---

[34] Heinrich Denzinger, "Sources of Catholic Dogma," English translation, older numbering, n.d. Retrieved September 27, 2020, from https://1ref.us/1dg.

[35] Gotthard Victor Lechler, *John Wycliffe and His English Precursors* (Religious Tract Society, 1904), 381.

[36] R. Shaw, *Papal Primacy in the Third Millennium* (Huntington, IN: Our Sunday Visitor, 2000). Retrieved September 27, 2020, from https://1ref.us/1dh.

Council of Lateran V, 1517 Holy Roman Empire

This was a significant council for church doctrine on opposition to teachings about death or what we call soul sleep and reaffirmed the doctrine of indulgences. The doctrines of the Catholic church hang on the existence of an immortal soul. If a person sleeps until the judgment where people go to heaven or hell, the whole concept of purgatory is null and void. No need to buy indulgences or come to the church for "graces" to help your relatives get out of purgatory. The church could not let this teaching on soul sleep continue. It is thought that if this council would have reigned in church and papal abuses, the Protestant Reformation may have been averted. Nevertheless, later that same year, Martin Luther would post his 99 Theses remonstrating the ecclesiastical abuses.

Council of Trent, 1563[37]

Trent is the "final nail in the coffin" council since it doubled down and codified all the previous non-biblical church teachings and erroneous doctrines in one council. Moreover, it attempted to counter Martin Luther's main emphasis on justification by faith alone. In the Catholic system, justification is doled out, little by little, through the seven sacraments. A sinner must come to the church where the priests dispense the merits of salvation. Luther's study of Scripture led him to discover that we are justified by faith alone because of Jesus' sacrifice on our behalf. Luther said, "The doctrine of Justification is this, that we are pronounced righteous and are saved solely by faith in Christ without works."[38] This short but concise statement threw out 1,000 years of papal teaching and dogma. No need for the seven sacraments to earn salvation. No need for priests to forgive sin or dole out grace piecemeal. No need to buy indulgences. No wonder Luther was vehemently hated, despised, and marked for death by the Roman Church!

> *The doctrine of Justification is this, that we are pronounced righteous and are saved solely by faith in Christ without works.*

---

37 "Canons and Decrees of the Council of Trent," Wikisource, November 24, 2016. Retrieved September 30, 2020, from https://1ref.us/1di.
38 Campbell & Satelmajer, *Here We Stand: Luther, the Reformation, and Seventh-day Adventism* (Nampa, ID: Pacific Press, 2017), 43.

Chapter 9:
Interpretation of Verses 23–39

Years of 508–ca 1453: Establishment of Church-State System in Europe (23–27)

23 And from the time that an alliance is made with him he shall act deceitfully, and he shall become strong with a small people.

YLT: And after they join themselves unto him, he worketh deceit, and hath increased, and hath been strong by a few of the nation.

The word "alliance" (ESV), "league" (KJV), or "join themselves" (YLT) comes from the Hebrew word *châbar*. Strong's definitions include: "to join (literally or figuratively); specifically (by means of spells) to fascinate:—charm(-er), be compact, couple (together), have fellowship with, heap up, join (self, together), league."[39] The definition does not indicate that this is any type of written, formal agreement as generally results from a peace treaty.

Some believe this alliance refers to the league the Jews was made with the Roman Republic in 161bc. Yet this would violate the rule of forward progression, and more importantly, this reaches beyond the age of the Roman Empire, which constituted the King of the North as the "Contemptable Person" found in verse 21. It would be a great stretch to say the Roman Republic is this Contemptable Person who transforms into the Papacy.

Starting at 476, after the fall of the Western Roman Empire, the Papacy had to make temporary alliances with its barbarian neighbors to survive. Nevertheless, the alliance with the Franks beginning in 508 would

---

39 H2266—chabar—Strong's Hebrew Lexicon (KJV), *Blue Letter Bible*, n.d. Retrieved September 27, 2020, from https://1ref.us/1dj.

not only be stronger than all the rest, would remain steadfast until the time appointed of 1798.

- While the previous alliances with Odoacer and the Ostrogoths were necessary for survival but short-lived, the most important alliance was between the Papacy and the Frankish kingdom. Unlike the Arian Theodoric of the Ostrogoths, Clovis I, after his baptism, declared Catholicism to be the state religion and subsequently forced all the people of the lands he conquered to convert. It is said, at the Battle of Tolbiac in 496, Clovis and his Franks were losing the battle, but he prayed to the God of his Catholic wife Clotilde and promised to become a Christian. Regarding the conversion of pagan nations in Western Europe, J.A. Wylie says, "[T]he Franks leading the way, and earning for themselves the title of the 'eldest son of the Church.'"[40]
- Importance of the Year 508:

  The Papacy after 476 was surrounded by Barbarian nations who were either pagan or Arian and often co-opted and manipulated Rome for their benefit. With Clovis conquering, enlarging his domain, and converting his subjects to Catholicism, the pope in Rome and the Emperor Anastasius in Constantinople took note of this powerful nation who could rid the western empire of the Arian and pagan barbarians which had plagued them since 476.

  ○ Gregory of Tours theatrical account of what happened in 508:

  Clovis received an appointment to the consulship from the emperor Anastasius, and in the church of the blessed Martin he clad himself in the purple tunic and chlamys, and placed a diadem on his head. Then he mounted his horse, and in the most generous manner he gave gold and silver as he passed along the way which is between the gate of the entrance [of the church of St. Martin] and the church of the city, scattering it among the people who were there with his own hand, and from that day he was called consul or Augustus. Leaving Tours he went to Paris and there he established the seat of his kingdom. There also Theodoric came to him.[41]

  Many historians question Gregory's account. However, what can be said for sure is Gregory and, by extent, the Catholic Church

---

40 J. A. Wylie, *The Papacy Is the Antichrist: A Demonstration* (Edinburgh: George M'Gibbon, 1888). Retrieved September 27, 2020, from https://1ref.us/1dk.

41 Saint Gregory & E. Brehaut, *History of the Franks* (New York: Octagon Books, 1965). Retrieved October 29, 2020, from https://1ref.us/1dl.

believed the account to be fact including "the wearing of the diadem was the operative act of succession that placed the seal of approval upon being hailed as Augustus."[42]

- ○ Based on the Battle of Vouillé in 507, Dr. Frank W. Hardy suggests the following events connected with Clovis occurred in 508:[43]
  - (a) Emperor Anastasius I Dicorus (491–518) gives Clovis an honorary consulship in celebration of his victory over Alaric.
  - (b) Clovis asserts his status as a conqueror by riding through the streets of Tours showering bystanders with coins.
  - (c) He eliminates a number of rival Frankish kings.
  - (d) He establishes his capital in Paris.
  - (e) He publishes a law code which had been in preparation earlier.
  - (f) Finally, on Christmas day, he accepts Catholic baptism at Tours, from the aged and saintly Bishop Remigius.
- With Clovis conquering Barbarian and Arian nations for the church and being bestowed the title of Imperial Roman Consul in the year 508, a 1290-year reign began with Catholicism as the official state religion of France until 1798. The Papacy was given a temporal power in 508 to enforce the emperor's letter of 533, which gave the Bishop of Rome all authority in the church, and finally, in 538, with the liberation of Rome from the last Arian nation, the popes had a dominion free from paganism and Arianism.

Christianity started small in Western Europe but took over the south-central portion of the cotenant by AD 600. However, even with an alliance with the Franks, the papal dominion was still basically confined to the city of Rome or this "small people" where the church was even under Ostrogothic control until General Belisarius cleared out the remaining Goths from the city in 538. The citizenry of Rome was still suffering from the barbarian sackings, war, and famine.

---

42   Mathisen, "Clovis," 97.
43   F. W. Hardy, "Clovis and the Year AD 508" (2016). Retrieved October 29, 2020, from https://1ref.us/1dm.

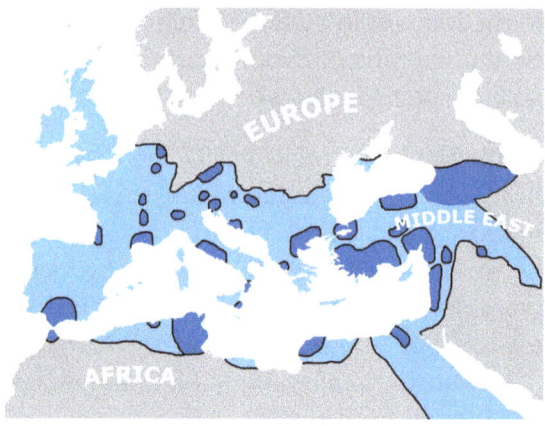

Christianity in AD 325 (Dark Blue) and AD 600 (Light Blue)[44]

Parallel text: 3 "Then a mighty king shall arise, who shall rule with great dominion and do as he wills."

The Papacy was, in fact, able to do precisely this, albeit, through planning, plotting, and schemes.

In Verse 23 we find our Missing Element in Daniel's Time Prophecies chart we looked at earlier. Since the 1290 and 1335 dates begin in the same year, 508, we can use this passage for our corresponding prophecy for both dates.

Time Prophecy	Corresponding Event Prophecy	Historical Event
"Time, times, and ½ a times" Daniel 7 and 12	Daniel 7:24 "As for the ten horns, out of this kingdom ten kings shall arise, and another shall arise after them" Daniel 7:26 "But the court shall sit in judgment, and his dominion shall be taken away, to be consumed and destroyed to the end."	This began in 538 when the Papacy had all three elements to rule Christendom: a temporal power arm (508 Frankish kingdom), authority (533 the letter from the Emperor), and domination to operate from (538 the defeat of the Ostrogoths from Rome). It ended in 1798 when the French Directory ordered General Berthier to capture and exile the pope removing his temporal authority.

---

44 "Christendom," Wikipedia, The Free Encyclopedia, 2020. Retrieved September 29, 2020, from https://1ref.us/1dn.

Time Prophecy	Corresponding Event Prophecy	Historical Event
2300 Days Daniel 8	Daniel 8:14, "And he said to me, "For 2,300 evenings and mornings. Then the sanctuary shall be restored to its rightful state."	This is the heavenly Day of Atonement which began 2,300 years from the Decree of Artaxerxes in 457 BC. In 1844, Jesus, our High Priest, entered the Most Holy Place in Heaven.
70 Weeks Daniel 9	Daniel 9:24, "Seventy weeks are decreed about your people and your holy city, to finish the transgression, to put an end to sin, and to atone for iniquity, to bring in everlasting righteousness, to seal both vision and prophet, and to anoint a most holy place.	Our starting point is the same as the 2300 Days with the decree Artaxerxes decree in 457 BC. Jesus started His earthly ministry in week 70 which was AD 27 at His baptism. In the middle of the week or in AD 31, He was crucified and ended the sacrificial service. Then in AD 34, at the end of the week, after Stephan's defense before the Jewish Sanhedrin, he was stoned and the 70-week probationary period for the Jews closed.
1290 Days Daniel 12	Daniel 11:23, "And from the time that an alliance is made with him he shall act deceitfully, and he shall become strong with a small people."	This time period links with Daniel 7 and the *time, times, and half of time* which ended in 1798, so if we move back 1290 year, we come to 508 and find an alliance with the king of the Franks and the Papacy that would last until 1798.
1335 Days Daniel 12	Daniel 11:23, "And from the time that an alliance is made with him he shall act deceitfully, and he shall become strong with a small people."	This time period links with Daniel 8 and the *2300 days* which ended in 1844. Daniel 12:12, "Blessed is he who waits and arrives at the 1,335 days." In 508 Catholicism was given a militant arm to carry out its anti-sanctuary ministry dogmas against God's true people. Even so, the year 1843 brought a blessing to God's people, free from papal persecution and a steadfast belief that Jesus was returning in the following year to "cleanse the sanctuary."

24 Without warning he shall come into the richest parts [among the richest men] of the province, and he shall do what neither his fathers nor

his fathers' fathers have done, scattering among them plunder, spoil, and goods. He shall devise plans against strongholds, but only for a time.

In 533 The Papacy began the process of receiving a temporal dominion.

The process of gaining land and temporal authority was a major goal of the Papacy throughout the early medieval times and by 756, he had the dominion Daniel was told about in chapter 7.

- Prior to 533, the only semi-independent property the Papacy had was the Lateran Palace, which was likely given by Constantine shortly after he "converted" in 312.
- In 533, the Duchy of Rome was provided to the Bishop of Rome even though it was officially ruled under the Byzantine Exarchate of Ravenna. With the expulsion of the Ostrogoths from Rome by General Belisarius in 538, the Papacy had a small dominion in Rome and the 1260-year prophecy began.
- In 728, the Donation of Sutri by the king of the Lombards formed the first extension of independent papal territory which was located on the border of the Duchy of Rome and contained the strategic fortified Castle of Sutri overlooking the road into Tuscany.
- In 756, the Donation of Pepin to the Papal States gave the Papacy a large independent section of central Italy running from Rome to Ravenna. This was based on an alliance with the Pepin the Short (or the Young) and the papacy. Pepin dethroned the last king of the Merovingian Dynasty and took the throne with the Catholic Church's blessing beginning the Carolingian Dynasty. Anointed by Pope Stephen II in 754, he then went to war against the Lombards, defeating them and donating their land to the Papacy. Pope Stephan may have used the forged Donation of Constantine in his appeal to Pepin to go against the Ostrogoths. Before the Lombards took the area, it was formerly the region controlled by the Byzantine Exarchate of Ravenna. Now the pope had a legal claim to an independent temporal kingdom of his own.

Simony, the practice of buying and selling ecclesiastical privileges, church offices, or promotion, began as early as 498.

Competing for the Papacy in 498, Symmachus and Laurentius both bribed Ostrogothic King Theodoric for his support to make them the pope using funds from the Roman aristocrats. Theodoric took both bribes, and they made Symmachus pope because he had more support than Laurentius. The final known act of the Roman Senate was a decree directed against simony, "shameless trafficking in sacred things was indulged in. Even sacred vessels were exposed for sale."[45]

The pope of Rome had to "devise plans" to be a temporal ruler, using monastic establishments to spread spiritual rule throughout Europe gaining leverage against the Emperor who had the Bishop of Constantinople at his side.

When Emperor Justinian I sent the famous letter to Pope John II giving him all ecumenical authority in the church,[46] the struggle from then on was not of the primacy church bishops, but rather it was a struggle for the primacy of Rome over Constantinople. Technically, the Bishop of Constantinople was under the pope, yet, the former had the emperor's ear while the emperor had the sword. This struggle of church-state power would continue until the pope had a stable, temporal militant army of his own.

"But only for a time" is a significant phrase. The word "time" used here is the Hebrew word `eth, and Strong's H6256 means "the time of an event." Hence the Papacy will engage in scattering plunder, spoil, and goods among those who honor them until the time of the end in 1798. Some believe the word "time" refers to the 360-year period between Battle of Actium in 33bc and the movement of the capitol of the Roman Empire to Constantinople. However, this word is never used for a 360 day for a year prophetic period. Additionally, Milan was the administrative capitol of the empire when it was moved to Constantinople. The Edit of Milan (313 AD) was so title because that was where Constantine's administrative capital was.

> Parallel text: 4 "And as soon as he has arisen, his kingdom shall be broken and divided toward the four winds of heaven, but not to his posterity, nor according to the authority with which he ruled, for his kingdom shall be plucked up and go to others besides these."
>
>> In 325 at the Council of Constantinople, Constantine divided his church up. Bishoprics of Rome, Constantinople, Antioch, and Alexandria. Constantine represented temporal authority, but the Bishoprics had ecclesiastical authority. By 650, only two bishoprics remained—Rome with its northern power-base in France and Constantinople with its southern power-base around the eastern Mediterranean.

---

45 Horace Kinder Mann, "Pope John II," *Catholic Encyclopedia* 8 (1913), Wikisource. Retrieved September 29, 2020, from https://1ref.us/1do.
46 "The Decrees of Justinian Declaring John, Bishop of Rome to be Chief Bishop of All the Churches [AD 533]," n.d. Retrieved September 27, 2020, from https://1ref.us/1dp.

25 And he shall stir up his power and his heart against the king of the south with a great army. And the king of the south shall wage war with an exceedingly great and mighty army, but he shall not stand, for plots shall be devised against him.

This describes the Gothic Wars of 535–554, ending all Arian opposition.

While prophecy was fulfilled in 508, 533, and 538, the last of the three kingdoms to be uprooted, continued to remain in northern Italy and this verse ties up that loose end.

The period between 493 and 537 is known as the Ostrogothic Papacy (KON). While the Ostrogoths were completely routed from Rome in 538, they were not totally defeated, and by 546 they had regrouped under King Totila with 15,000 men and had briefly retaken Rome. In 551, Justinian sent General Narses (KOS) with a force of almost 30,000 men. In 552 at the Battle of Taginae Northeast of Rome, Narses and his army defeated the Ostrogoths, killed King Totila, and liberated Rome. Finally, at the Battle of Mons Lactarius, the new king, Theia, was killed. The army was vanquished, and the remaining Ostrogothic populace fled back to the region of Austria and was absorbed there with the Lombards who would later occupy the peninsula.

A note about "north" and "south," the original "King of the North," King of Selucia, was practically due east of Palestine, and Imperial Rome was more west than north. Egypt was not due south of Palestine, but southwest. In our current text, the King of the South moves from the south up the Italian peninsula to attack towards the north.

As to "plots shall be devised against him," this can be seen in the fact that the Papacy initially supported the Ostrogoths and the subsequent interplay among the popes, Ostrogoths, and the emperor.

- In 523, Pope John I traveled to Constantinople on behalf of Ostrogoth King Theodoric to see Emperor Justin I about his decree against Arian beliefs and plead for better treatment of the Ostrogoths. Upon John's return, Theodoric had him imprisoned at Ravenna for conspiring with the emperor where he later died.
- Between 530 and 532, Boniface II an Ostrogoth occupied the Papacy and was elected because of the influence of Ostrogoth King Athalaric.
- In 536, Pope Agapetus I traveled to Constantinople on behalf of Ostrogoth King Theodahad to get the emperor to cancel Belisarius's preparation for the invasion of the Italian Peninsula. Justinian immediately refused, and the pope dropped that matter altogether

and moved to a Papal supremacy issue—the Bishop of Constantinople, which was doubtless the real reason for his taking the journey to the capital. The pope believed the Bishop to be a heretic, but Justinian supported the appointment. When Justinian threatened Agapetus with banishment, he is reported to have stated, "With eager longing have I come to gaze upon the Most Christian Emperor Justinian. In his place, I find a Diocletian, whose threats, however, terrify me not."[47] Agapetus appeared to be more lenient to the Arians, by allowing them to convert to Catholicism but only as laymen and not Bishops or priests.
- In 536, Pope Silverius approved Belisarius's entrance into Rome. Richards states, "What followed is as tangled a web of treachery and double-dealing as can be found anywhere in the papal annals. Several different versions of the course of events following the elevation of Silverius exist."[48] Silverius was accused by Belisarius of conspiring with the Ostrogoth and deposed in 537.
- In 537, Pope Vigilius became pope with the support of Belisarius and Empress Theodora. Even so, this did not end well for Vigilius due to the Three Chapters Controversy.
- In 556, Pope Pelagius I was selected pope by Justinian. He promptly reversed Pope Vigilius's condemnation of the Three Chapters.

Parallel Text: 5 "Then the king of the south shall be strong, but one of his princes shall be stronger than he and shall rule, and his authority shall be a great authority."

>Theodoric was a captive in Constantinople (KOS) but was commissioned by Emperor Zeno to capture and dethrone Odoacer and in return, his people the Ostrogoths (KON) could settle in the Italian Peninsula by 493.

26 Even those who eat his food shall break him. His army shall be swept away, and many shall fall down slain.

The Ostrogoths had given the Roman Papacy limited temporal power against Constantinople for a short time. The populace of the peninsula had been devastated by war, famine, and disease. Ravenna was at this time the Byzantine capital of the west. Also, the Papacy had lost control over papal elections and entered the period called the Byzantine Papacy which lasted until 742 with Pope Zachary the last pope to seek approval

---
[47] James Francis Loughlin, "Pope St. Agapetus I," in *Catholic Encyclopedia* 1, ed. Charles Herbermann (New York: Robert Appleton Company, 1907).
[48] Jeffrey Richards, *The Popes and the Papacy in the Early Middle Ages*, 476–752 (London; Boston: Routledge and Kegan Paul, 1979) 129.

from the Byzantine Emperor. The Papacy would not gain the upper hand on Constantinople until 800 with the crowning of Charlemagne.

Parallel text: 6 "After some years they shall make an alliance, and the daughter of the king of the south shall come to the king of the north to make an agreement. But she shall not retain the strength of her arm, and he and his arm shall not endure, but she shall be given up, and her attendants, he who fathered her, and he who supported her in those times."

From 775 to 780, Irene was the Byzantine empress by marriage to Emperor Leo IV. When he died, she became co-regent with her son Constantine VI to 797 when she blinded her son and had him dethroned. She was the sole ruler and first empress regnant of the Byzantine Empire from 797 to 802. The Pope refused to recognize her because she was a woman. Theophanes the Confessor states that Irene endeavored to bring about a marriage alliance between herself and Charlemagne Emperor of the Holy Roman Empire. The plan was upset by her trusted advisor, Aetius. In 802, the nobles in Constantinople dethroned and exiled her, placing Nikephoros as emperor.

27 And as for the two kings, their hearts shall be bent on doing evil. They shall speak lies at the same table, but to no avail, for the end is yet to be at the time appointed.

711 Pope Constantine traveled to Constantinople to end a dispute over the Quinisext Ecumenical Council controversy.

Originally, Pope Sergius I rejected the Quinisext Ecumenical Council, was later ordered to be arrested, and brought to Constantinople by Justinian II. He was protected in Ravenna by its militia and died in 701. Neither of the next two popes ratified the council.

Emperor Justinian II officially commanded that Pope Constantine appear in Constantinople regarding the Quinisext Ecumenical Council. While the pope went without delay, his real motive was the split over sacramental marriages. He ratified the council and returned to Rome in 711.

In the negotiations, a compromise was reached where Pope Constantine gave ground on Economia or the handling, management, and disposition of the council, but he held firm on most other papal concerns. It was a compromise borne of diplomatic speak where many words were spoken but accomplished little towards ending the rift between the two parties. This would be the last visit of a pope to Constantinople and the Orthodox Church until 1967.

> Parallel text: 7 "And from a branch from her roots one shall arise in his place. He shall come against the army and enter the fortress of the king of the north, and he shall deal with them and shall prevail."
>
>> Irene's legacy in the East was her anti-Iconoclasm attitude which she hid from the Emperor during the first Iconoclast period of 730–787. However, as regent, she promoted image veneration. During the second iconoclast period of 814-843, Empress Theodora, whose life nearly mirrors that of Irene, led the restoration of image and icon veneration and ended the Byzantine opposition for good.

28 And he shall return to his land with great wealth, but his heart shall be set against the holy covenant. And he shall work his will and return to his own land.

After 756 and the establishment of the Papal States, the territories of the Italian Peninsula gave direct temporal sovereign rule to the pope.

The papacy was able to work her will using the counterfeit Donation of Constantine, arguing that if Constantine the Great had previously granted this land to the Papacy, then the land of Donation of Pepin was rightfully hers. Cairns in his book Christianity Through the Centuries gives this description of the Donation of Constantine:

> In the document Constantine greets Sylvester and the bishops of the church and went on to relate that he had been healed of leprosy and baptized by Sylvester. In return, he declared that the church at Rome was to have precedence over all other churches and that its bishop was the supreme bishop in the church. He gave territories throughout his empire, the Lateran Palace, and the clothing and insignia of the imperial rank to Sylvester. Constantine then withdrew to Constantinople so that he would not interfere with the imperial rights of the pope.[49]

787 2nd Council of Nicaea—Approved idol worship and Tradition over Scripture

Thus, we find the first time an ecumenical council confirming that Christians must adhere not only to the faith of the Church but also to its traditional practices. This is clearly set out in the anathemas[50] that follow from the council:

---

[49] E. Cairns, Christianity Through the Centuries: A History of the Christian Church (Grand Rapids, MI: Zondervan, 1954), 183.

[50] N. P. Tanner, ed., "Second Council of Nicaea—787 A.D.," in *Decrees of the Ecumenical Councils* (Washington, DC: Georgetown University Press, 1990). Retrieved September 27, 2020, from https://1ref.us/1dq.

- If anyone does not confess that Christ our God can be represented in His humanity, let him be anathema.
- If anyone does not accept representation in art of evangelical scenes, let him be anathema.
- If anyone does not salute such representations as standing for the Lord and His saints, let him be anathema.
- If anyone rejects any written or unwritten tradition of the Church, let him be anathema.

Pope Adrian I consolidated papal power, had a wide-ranging domestic policy, and rebuilt Rome's infrastructure, including aqueducts and basilicas. He reigned for 22 years and died in 795.

Parallel text: 8 "He shall also carry off to Egypt their gods with their metal images and their precious vessels of silver and gold, and for some years he shall refrain from attacking the king of the north."

> The Pope and the western Catholicism began venerating images and icons early in church history, but this practice was discouraged in the Eastern churches.
>
> The Eastern churches were champions of Iconoclasm with the objective of destroying icons and other images or monuments, which was and a major issue with the Western Catholic Church.
>
> The church in Constantinople, supported by the emperor, outlawed icons in the east but left alone the church in the west. In 754, Emperor Constantine V forbade venerations of icons throughout the whole empire. However, in 787, the Second Council of Nicaea restored the veneration of icons and images throughout the whole church.

29 At the time appointed he shall return and come into the south, but it shall not be this time as it was before.

The Pope as KON attacked Constantinople as KOS again, but this time as a temporal power and not through a Barbarian tribe.

The Exarchate of Ravenna, a Byzantine Empire land-holding, was captured by Pepin. Pope Adrian I authorized Charlemagne to take away anything from Ravenna that he liked, which he took an unknown quantity of Roman columns, mosaics, statues, and other portable items north to enrich his capital of Aachen. Ravenna then gradually came under the direct authority of the Popes; although, the archbishops contested this at various times.

With the crowning of Charlemagne by Pope Leo III, the Byzantines and Franks (Holy Romans) were in a cold war. Unlike the previous hot war in verse 25 where the King of the South, through Narses, came with an overwhelming army, this time Charlemagne as the King of the North, with sizable force, attacked the Byzantine peripheral states of Venice and the Dalmatian coast similar to the US involvement in Southeast Asia against the Communists. The Byzantines were not in a position to send a large force to their aid.

Cairns gives this report:

> Considerable emphasis should be given to the influence of Charlemagne in medieval history. His coronation marked the reconciliation and union of the population of the old Roman Empire with the Teutonic conquer. It ended the dream of the Eastern emperor to regain for the Eastern segment of the Roman Empire the areas lost to the barbarians in the West in the fifth century. Because the pope had crowned Charlemagne, his position was enhanced as one to whom rulers owed their crowns; and the emperor was bound to aid him when he was in difficulty. Charlemagne's coronation marked the peak of Frankish power that began with Clovis' decision to become a Christian.[51]

In addition to Charlemagne's advances in the Byzantium west, the pope refused to acknowledge Irene as Byzantine Emperor in 797. At this time, the Byzantines defended the east of the empire against the Arabs and could not devote much effort against the Franks.

In 811, a peace treaty was finally signed between Charlemagne and Byzantine Emperor Michael I where the Byzantine Empire would accept Charlemagne as king of the Franks, and he gave back the Dalmatian coast region. On the other hand, the Venetians allied with the Franks possibly to free themselves from Byzantine control.

Parallel text: 9 "Then the latter shall come into the realm of the king of the south but shall return to his own land."

Charlemagne entered the territories of Byzantine of northeast Italy and the Balkan Peninsula but soon returned to his kingdom land.

30 For ships of Kittim shall come against him, and he shall be afraid and withdraw, and shall turn back and be enraged and take action against the holy covenant. He shall turn back and pay attention to those who forsake the holy covenant.

Out of their Mediterranean Sea bases, Arab pirate raiders sacked Rome in 843, which caused the Papacy to form the Italian League of Papal,

---
51   Cairns, *Christianity*, 188.

Neapolitan, Amalfitan, and Gaetan ships to fend off the Arab pirates winning the famous naval Battle of Ostia in 849.

There has been much debate over where Kittim is located. In fact, the Septuagint uses Rome here instead of Kittem. While it is known that the physical location is on the Island of Cyprus, no historical account fits this prophetic description. Some have seen Kittem as a description of all Mediterranean islands in general. The Jewish Encyclopedia states, "Nevertheless the term 'isles of Kittim' (Jer. ii. 10; Ezek. xxvii. 6) indicates that "Kittim" signified all the islands and coastlands of the West, and, according to I Macc. i. 1 (ΧΧεττείμ) and viii. 5 (Καρραιτέων βασιλέα), included Macedonia, and, according to Dan. xi. 30, even Italy."[52]

Originally protected by the Byzantine navy, Rome found itself in need of a naval force of their own following the Muslim raid on Rome in 843 and the sack of Old St Peter's and St Paul's-Outside-the-Walls basilicas in 846. The Italian league of Papal, Neapolitan, Amalfitan, and Gaetan ships fended off the Muslim pirates during the naval Battle of Ostia in 849.

The Battle of Ostia—by Raphael[53]

---

52 R. Gottheil & S. Krauss, "Cyprus," *Jewish Encyclopedia* (1906). Retrieved September 27, 2020, from https://1ref.us/1dr.
53 Raphael, "Ostia." Wikimedia Commons, the free media repository. Retrieved September 29, 2020, from https://1ref.us/1ds.

The Covenant was attacked with sanctioning idolatry and veneration of Mary.

In 870, the Fourth Council of Constantinople declared:

> We decree that the sacred image of our Lord Jesus Christ, the liberator and Savior of all people, must be venerated with the same honor as is given the book of the holy Gospels. For as through the language of the words contained in this book all can reach salvation, so, due to the action which these images exercise by their colors, all wise and simple alike, can derive profit from them. For what speech conveys in words, pictures announce and bring out in colors.[54]

If anyone does not venerate the image of Christ our Lord, let him be deprived of seeing him in glory at his second coming. The image of his all-pure Mother and the images of the holy angels as well as the images of all the saints are equally the object of our homage and veneration.[55]

However, early in church history, Mary's worship was condemned by many. Near the end of the 4th century, Epiphanius of Salamis made the following declaration:

> For I have heard in turn that others who are out of their minds on this subject of this holy Ever-virgin, have done their best and are doing their best, in the grip both of madness and of folly, to substitute her for God. For they say that certain Thracian women there in Arabia have introduced this nonsense, and that they bake a loaf in the name of the Ever-virgin, gather together, and attempt an excess and undertake a forbidden, blasphemous act in the holy Virgin's name, and offer sacrifice in her name with women officiants.
>
> This is entirely impious, unlawful, and different from the Holy Spirit's message, and is thus pure devil's work...
>
> And nowhere was a woman a priest. But I shall go to the New Testament. If it were ordained by God that women should be priests or have any canonical function in the Church, Mary herself, if anyone, should have functioned as a priest in the New Testament. She was counted worthy to bear the king of all in her own womb, the heavenly God, the Son of God. Her womb became a temple, and by God's kindness and an awesome mystery, was prepared to be a

---

54 Gesa Elsbeth Thiessen, *Theological Aesthetics: A Reader* (Grand Rapids, MI: William B. Eerdmans Publishing Company, 2005), 65.
55 Steven Bigham, *Image of God the Father in Orthodox Theology and Iconography* (Oakwood Publications, 1995), 41.

dwelling place of the Lord's human nature. But it was not God's pleasure that she be a priest.[56]

Parallel text: 10 "His sons shall wage war and assemble a multitude of great forces, which shall keep coming and overflow and pass through, and again shall carry the war as far as his fortress."

With the victory over Iconoclasm, the Popes from this point on dominated the ecclesiastical authority in the church, and only one more church council was held in the East.

Parallel text: 11 "Then the king of the south, moved with rage, shall come out and fight against the king of the north. And he shall raise a great multitude, but it shall be given into his hand."

During the Photian Schism of 863–867, the church in Constantinople challenged the authority of the Pope. The issue centered around the Byzantine Emperor's right to depose and appoint a patriarch without approval from the Papacy. Emperor Michael III deposed the Bishop of Constantinople and replaced him with another. The Council of Constantinople of 861 approved the actions of the emperor but was rejected by the pope. In the end, Pope Nicholas died, the emperor was assassinated, and the Fourth Council of Constantinople convened to end the schism.

31 Forces from him shall appear and profane the temple and fortress, and shall take away the regular burnt offering. And they shall set up the abomination that makes desolate.

YTL 31 And strong ones out of him stand up, and have polluted the sanctuary, the stronghold, and have turned aside the continual [sacrifice], and appointed the desolating abomination.

Some scholars, principally Uriah Smith, see this as the starting point for the Frankish-Papal alliance started by Clovis I in 508. It is undoubtedly true that this verse is speaking of the power of the Papacy to take away the "daily/continual." Even so, there appears to be no indication in the texts itself that this is a transition from Imperial Rome in verse 30 to Papal Rome in this verse. The *SDA Bible Commentary* suggests the "forces" or "arms" come from the Papacy's "sanctuary of strength" either from the city of Rome itself or against the heavenly sanctuary. With this text's focus being the Papacy and the sanctuary, there is little to suggest the text refers to Clovis I or the Frankish-Papal alliance. Furthermore, while the Franks in 508 converted conquered people—pagans and Arians—to Catholicism in a general sense, they were by no means enforcing Papal dogma with the sword.

---

56 Tim Staples, "The Assumption of Mary in History,"*Catholic Magazine Online* (August 12, 2019). Retrieved September 29, 2020, from https://1ref.us/1dt.

Interpretation of Verses 23–39

By sending the secular powers to enforce the dogmas of the church, the abomination of desolation was set up.

The Pope's "forces" were the temporal powers in Europe, the increased focus of the inquisition beginning in the 1250s[57] and later with the Jesuit Order beginning in 1540.[58] These forces began to attack God's people after the Third Council of Lateran in 1179 with the condemnation of Waldensianism and Albigensianism.

The Waldensians' beliefs included: the atoning death and justifying righteousness of Christ, the Godhead, the fall of man, the incarnation of the Son, denied the existence of purgatory, voluntary poverty, opposed the authority of the state and the Church, and opposed the sacrament of matrimony. The Albigensians believed the Catholic priesthood was not needed, and they rejected the idea that the real presence of Christ was in the Eucharist and denied the existence of purgatory.

Through the Eucharist and the Sacraments, the Daily/Continual offering was taken away.

At the Fourth Council of Lateran in 1215, it was ordered that parishioners must keep the annual reception of penance and the Eucharist. They also used the term "transubstantiation" to explain the Real Presence of Christ in the Eucharist.

There is a completely different meaning between the Protestant communion service and the Catholic Eucharist mass. Malachi Martin in his massive work, *The Keys to This Blood*, explains:

> When you talk of the Eucharist, you are talking about the Roman Mass, which has been and still is the central act of worship for Roman Catholics. The value of the Mass for Catholics is twofold. A Mass, in the Catholic belief, represents the real live Sacrifice of the body and blood and physical life of Jesus consummated on Calvary. It is not a commemoration of that sacrifice, nor a reenactment after the fashion of a historical drama, nor a symbolic performance.
>
> Therein lies the mystery of the Mass. When a Roman Mass is said to be valid, it is believed to achieve that mysterious presentation

> *There is a completely different meaning between the Protestant communion service and the Catholic Eucharist mass.*

---

57 "Inquisition," History.com (2017). Retrieved September 29, 2020, from https://1ref.us/1du.
58 "Jesuit Order Established," History.com (2010). Retrieved September 29, 2020, from https://1ref.us/1dv.

of Christ's sacrifice of his bodily life. It has validity; and Roman Catholics can then literally adore their Savior under the physical appearance of the bread and wine.[59]

In the Old Testament, the regular priests ministered in the courtyard and the holy place doing the "continual/daily" duties. While the high priest supervised the workings in the courtyard and the holy place of the sanctuary, only he could enter the most holy place and only one day per year. God's New Testament people are a holy and royal priesthood of believers.[60] Martin Luther also believed this to be the case and that priesthood of believers flowed through Jesus where Christians are to perform the basic duties of the Levitical priesthood.[61]

In an article from Amazing Facts *Inside Report* titled "Secrets of the Sanctuary," the plan of salvation through the sanctuary is explained in concise, yet vivid, detail.

> "The sanctuary consisted of three principal areas: the courtyard, the holy place, and the most holy place. These three locations represent the three primary steps in the process of salvation known as justification, sanctification, and glorification, and they correspond with three phases of Christ's ministry: the substitutionary sacrifice, the priestly mediation, and the final judgment."[62]

---

[59] Malachi Martin, *The Keys to this Blood: Pope John Paul II Versus Russia and the West for the Control of the New World Order* (New York: Touchstone, 1990), 667.
[60] 1 Pet. 2:5, 9.
[61] Campbell & Satelmajer, *"Here We Stand,"* 36, 37.
[62] "Secrets of the Sanctuary," Amazing Facts, *Inside Report* (2018). Retrieved September 29, 2020, from https://1ref.us/1dw.

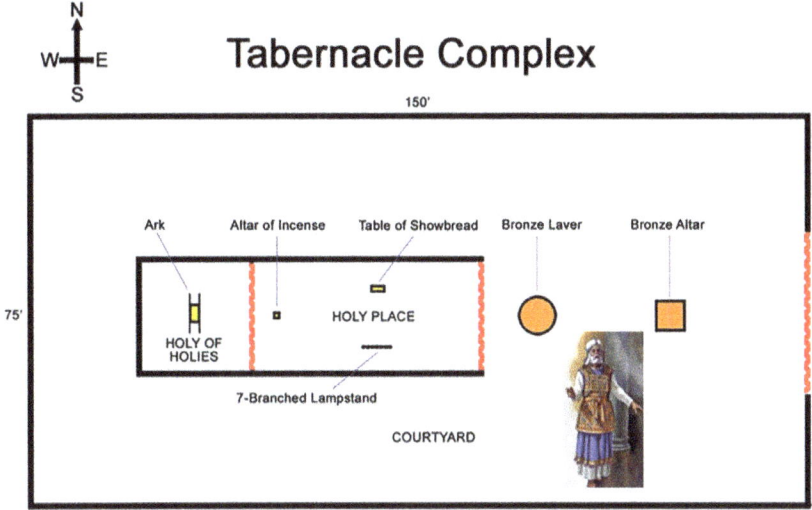

- Symbolically in the Courtyard we are justified and have:
  - accepted Jesus who was sacrificed once for all.
  - been baptized into his death and resurrection.
- We are now able to enter the Holy Place of the Sanctuary to spiritually perform the "continual/daily" duties of a priest:
  - before the Altar of Incense with our personal and corporate prayers.
  - before the Table of Showbread through Bible study and devotions.
  - before the Lampstand letting our light shine through our Fruit of the Spirit and our Gift(s) of the Spirit.
- Finally, we are ministers at the curtain separating the Holy from the Most Holy place:
  - symbolically sprinkling the blood of Jesus trusting in His merits as our Sacrifice and High Priest to provide us mercy and give us the strength to keep His commandments; thus, we emulate His character of love in our lives and are being prepared for glorification at His soon coming.

However, the Catholic Church has replaced our priestly Daily/Continual duties in the Sanctuary with the Eucharist and the Seven Sacraments.

- In the Courtyard:
  - Jesus is continually sacrificed in the Mass, and attendance is a sacrament to help earn salvation.
  - Baptism is by sprinkling, and it is also a sacrament.
- In the Holy Place of the Sanctuary:

- Tradition replaced Scripture, and only the church can interpret the Bible.
- Praying the Rosary and Prayers are to Mary and the Saints.
- Only priests can teach and bring others into the church.
* In the Most Holy Place:
  - Mercy is dispensed by the church, and specifically, Mary is the Mother of Mercy.[63]
  - The Ten Commandments were changed into the character of the Papacy with the removal of the second commandment allowing for idolatry, then shortening of the fourth to just: "Remember to keep holy the Sabbath day" and transferring the solemnity of the Sabbath to Sunday, and finally making the tenth commandment into two commandments to maintain "Ten" Commandments.

God's people are priests in the holy place of the sanctuary, but in the Catholic Church, only their priests can enter the holy place. They dispense salvation piecemeal through the seven sacraments to the parishioners. (See Appendix C for further study on the Continual Sanctuary Ministry and the desecration of the sanctuary service.)

Parallel text: 12 "And when the multitude is taken away, his heart shall be exalted, and he shall cast down tens of thousands, but he shall not prevail."

In 1453, Constantinople fell to the Ottoman Empire, and the multitude of opponents to Papal supremacy ended. The Council of Trent in 1563 cemented all the errors of the church, and the church persecuted anyone would not follow their dogmas. Catholicism would not prevail because, within 250 years, their church-state system would be replaced with an atheistic-state system in France and a Protestant separation of church and state system in America.

Years of ca 1209–1798: Protestant Revolution verses 32–35

(Aside from the specific dates of 1209–1798, several contemporary scholars see these verses representing overall religious persecution and the Protestant Reformation, including: Zdravko Stefanovic, Tim Roosenberg, and Norman McNulty.)

32 He shall seduce with flattery those who violate the covenant, but the people who know their God shall stand firm and take action

---

63 Robert Stackpole, "Why Do We Call Mary 'Mother of Mercy,'" The Divine Mercy, January 16, 2016. Retrieved September 29, 2020, from https://1ref.us/1dx.

Parallel text: 13 "For the king of the north shall again raise a multitude, greater than the first. And after some years he shall come on with a great army and abundant supplies."

Suggested Interpretation: Those who violate the covenant are those who choose to accept tradition and church dogma over Scripture.

Malachi Martin reflects on the medieval Papacy stating, "During the first thousand years of Christian papal Rome as a visible power among men–from 400 to 1400 AD–the Roman papacy and its ecclesiastical structure, the Church, were the fashioners of the Western culture and tradition."[64]

This "flattery" or smooth things can be seen in the praise for Pope Pius V standardized the Mass in the Roman Missal, which was produced in1570 after the entreaty of the Council of Trent of 1563. Pope Pius issued the *Quo primum* (from the first) papal Bull making his missal mandatory throughout the Catholic Church and has remained essentially unchanged for 400 years.

The Catholic church worked hand-in-hand with the Habsburg Dynasty against the Protestant Reformation overtly in Spain and Italy and likewise, covertly using the Jesuits in Central Europe. According to the "World of the Habsburg" website "the goal of making the mass of the population return to the Catholic Church was achieved not only by intensified pastoral care and pious works, but also through terror and violence. Habsburg state power rigorously destroyed Protestant ecclesiastical structures and persecuted non-Catholics mercilessly."[65]

Shortly after the Third Council of Lateran in 1209, the French military under the orders of Pope Innocent III began the Albigensian or Cather Crusade which lasted for 20 years. Many were ordered to wear yellow crosses on their outer clothes, imprisoned, lost property, and were burned. On March 16, 1244, a massacre of over 200 were burned in a massive pyre.

There are many of God's true people who rightly fit the descrip-

Luther risked almost certain death for his challenge to the medieval establishment. But he was a man under conviction and moved forward despite the religious and civil powers arrayed against him.

---
64 Martin, *The Keys*, 501.
65 M. Mutschlechner, "The Struggle for People's Souls—the Habsburgs and the Counter-Reformation," The World of Habsburgs, n.d. Retrieved September 29, 2020, from https://1ref.us/1dy.

tion of "shall stand firm and take action." While not the first nor the last, Martin Luther aptly fits this description. Dr. George Knight says by nailing his 95 Theses to the church door at Wittenberg, Luther's propositions "soon jumped the fence of separating the academic world from that of personal Christian piety and politics, and they ignited a revolution – a Reformation. Luther risked almost certain death for his challenge to the medieval establishment. But he was a man under conviction and moved forward despite the religious and civil powers arrayed against him."[66]

33 And the wise among the people shall make many understand, though for some days they shall stumble by sword and flame, by captivity and plunder.

Parallel text: 14 "In those times many shall rise against the king of the south, and the violent among your own people shall lift themselves up in order to fulfill the vision, but they shall fail."

In 1553, Queen (Bloody) Mary I ascended to the English throne and attempted to mend the relationship between the English church and Rome. She repealed all religious legislation passed under Edward VI, and many Protestants were exiled, imprisoned, burned at the stake, tortured, or punished in other ways. The Wikipedia article states, *"Foxe's Book of Martyrs* offers an account of the executions, which extended well beyond the anticipated targets—high-level clergy. Tradesmen were also burned, as well as married men and women, sometimes in unison, 'youths' and at least one couple was burned alive with their daughter. The figure of 300 victims of the Marian Persecutions was given by Foxe and later by Thomas Brice in his poem, 'The Regester.'"[67]

34 When they stumble, they shall receive a little help. And many shall join themselves to them with flattery,

Many Catholics sympathizers in Protestant areas joined with the Protestants to avoid conflict.

With the full authority of the Pope and the Council of Trent, the church persecuted and burned at the stake millions who would not succumb to their edicts and dictates of the Pope.

In 1570 Pope Pius V codified all the previous developments in a new Eucharist missal, which became the standard for the Western Church.

Malachi Martin describes this mystery of the Eucharist in great detail: "In the Roman Church, this mystery was celebrated in the Roman Mass,

---

66 Campbell & Satelmajer, *Here We Stand*, 9.
67 "List of Protestant Martyrs of the English Reformation," Wikipedia, The Free Encyclopedia, 2020. Retrieved September 29, 2020, from https://1ref.us/1dz.

a liturgical ceremony that attained its traditional form in the early Middle Ages, was confirmed as a perpetual law in 1570 by Pope Pius V, and was recognized at the Council of Trent in the same century."[68]

The Council of Trent in 1563 upheld tradition, stated salvation was not by "faith alone," decreed the Mass as a real sacrifice, defended purgatory, indulgences, the jurisdiction of the pope, and initiated the Counter-Reformation;

Parallel text: 15 "Then the king of the north shall come and throw up siegeworks and take a well-fortified city. And the forces of the south shall not stand, or even his best troops, for there shall be no strength to stand."

35 and some of the wise shall stumble, so that they may be refined, purified, and made white, until the time of the end, for it still awaits the appointed time.

Reason sees recantation as a normal strategy used by reformers to avoid death.[69] Copernicus, while his scientific discoveries were in a direct contradiction that Rome was the center of the solar system, quietly bowed to church dogma. However, a contemporary of Copernicus, Galileo faced the Inquisitorial commission by Pope Paul V and was forced to write out his recantation. "I, Galileo, son of the late Vincenzo Galilei, Florentine, aged seventy years, arraigned personally before this tribunal, and kneeling before you, Most Eminent and Reverend Lord Cardinals, Inquisitors-General against heretical depravity throughout the entire Christian commonwealth, having before my eyes and touching with my hands, the Holy Gospels, swear that I have always believed, do believe, and by God's help will in the future believe, all that is held, preached, and taught by the Holy Catholic and Apostolic Church."[70]

"[U]ntil the time of the end, for it still awaits the appointed time" is another specific reference to the time of the end in 1798. When will the persecution of the Dark Ages end? In 1798 when the Papacy loses its temporal power.

---

68   Martin, *The Keys*, 667.
69   A. Reason, "Sincere Lies and Creative Truth: Recantation Strategies During the English Reformation," *Journal of History and Cultures* 1 (2012): 1–18. Retrieved September 29, 2020, from https://1ref.us/1e0.
70   Giorgio de Santillana, "Recantation of Galileo (June 22, 1633)," in *The Crime of Galileo* (Chicago: Chicago University Press, 1955), 312, 313. Retrieved September 29, 2020, from https://1ref.us/1e1.

Years of 1453–1798: Full Power and Authority of the Papacy verses 36–39

(Much of this section follows the predominant SDA interpretation and that found in McNulty.[71])

36 "And the king shall do as he wills. He shall exalt himself and magnify himself above every god, and shall speak astonishing things against the God of gods. He shall prosper till the indignation is accomplished; for what is decreed shall be done."

Parallel text: 16 "But he who comes against him shall do as he wills, and none shall stand before him. And he shall stand in the glorious land, with destruction in his hand."

The Papacy here reached the height of its power. He now heads the only Christian church-state system with the fall of Constantinople. He can make political rulers conform to their wishes by threat of excommunication. He uses his state power to persecute the Protestants. And finally, through his councils, edicts, he has attacked the holy covenant by controverting the plan of salvation; instituting the Eucharist; profaning and replacing the daily sanctuary service by instituting the rosary, prayers to Mary and the saints; forbidding the reading and possession of the Bible; instituting a system of salvation by works; and changing God's commandments—removing the 2nd which allowed worship image and replacing the 4th with Sunday worship. The Papacy continued until 1798 when the indignation against him reached its fill.

---

[71] Norman McNulty, *Commentary on the Book of Daniel: Practical Living in the Judgement Hour* (Coldwater, MI: Remnant Publishing, 2019), 222–226.

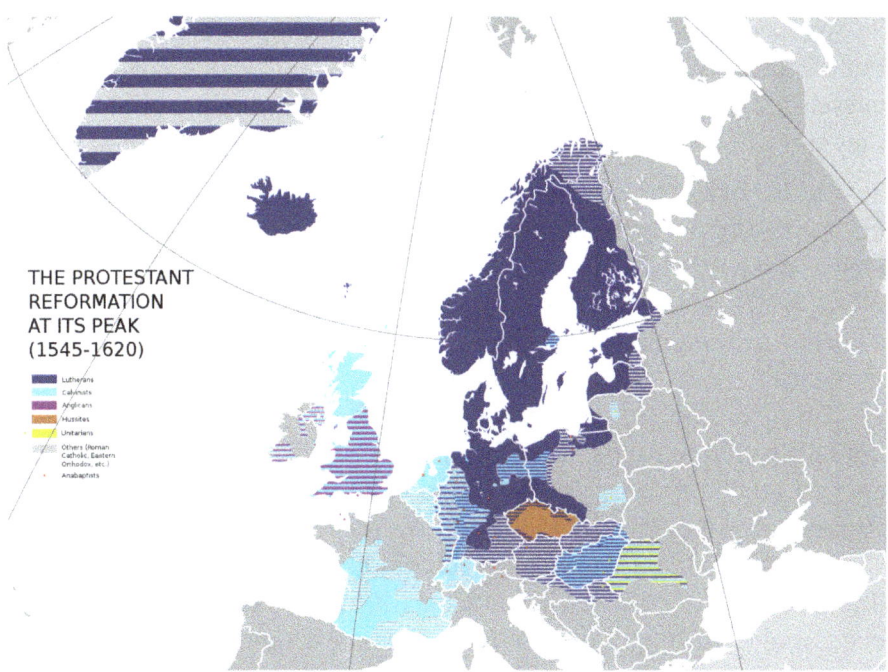

Religions in Europe mid-1600th Century[72]

37 He shall pay no attention to the gods of his fathers, or to the one beloved by women. He shall not pay attention to any other god, for he shall magnify himself above all.

Parallel text: 17 "He shall set his face to come with the strength of his whole kingdom, and he shall bring terms of an agreement and perform them. He shall give him the daughter of women to destroy the kingdom, but it shall not stand or be to his advantage."

Here we see the Papacy elevating tradition and councils over the Bible, the Word of God, and promoting celibacy. In the mid-16th century, Pope Pius V stated, "The Pope and God are the same, so he has all power in Heaven and earth."[73]

This "god his fathers did not know" refers to traditions, council canons, and papal bulls that have come in and replaced the Word of God. To the early church, a "thus sayeth the Lord" came from an apostle or the Old Testament Scriptures. Acts 15: 21 is clear, "For from ancient generations Moses (the Torah) has had in every city those who proclaim him, for he is read every Sabbath in the synagogues."

---

72 "Protestant Reformation," Map, Wikimedia Commons, retrieved October 29, 2020, from https://1ref.us/1e2.

73 quoted in W. Barclay, De potestate papae: an, et quatenus in Reges et Principes seculares jus et imperium habeat (1609) chapter 27, 218. Retrieved January 7, 2021, from https://1ref.us/1hj ..

While celibacy was a part of the church dating back to 304, in 1074, Pope Gregory VII was the champion of priestly celibacy with his published encyclical forbidding the priests and clergy from marrying and command they stay celibate.[74]

38 He shall honor the god of fortresses instead of these. A god whom his fathers did not know he shall honor with gold and silver, with precious stones and costly gifts.

Parallel text: 18 "Afterward he shall turn his face to the coastlands and shall capture many of them, but a commander shall put an end to his insolence. Indeed, he shall turn his insolence back upon him."

This god of fortresses can be seen in the temporal power of the pope not only with the Jesuits, Dominicans, and Papal Army but with the powers of Catholic nations. Instead of using a "thus sayeth the Lord," the Papacy uses a "thus sayeth the blade."[75]

Tim Roosenberg describes these "god of fortresses" as the "cathedrals, which have become their trademark, and the cathedrals have often been used as fortresses during times of war. The god the fathers did not know would be the worship of Mary decorated with gold, precious stones, and pleasant things. Just think of the statues of Mary and how they are decorated."[76]

39 He shall deal with the strongest fortresses with the help of a foreign god. Those who acknowledge him he shall load with honor. He shall make them rulers over many and shall divide the land for a price [payment].

Parallel text: 19 Then he shall turn his face back toward the fortresses of his own land, but he shall stumble and fall, and shall not be found.

Some see this "foreign god" as Mary and her being the Co-Redemtrix with Jesus along with the belief she was taken to heaven without sin.

We see this distribution of land for a price in the church's property holdings throughout the world. Also, in 1493, Pope Alexander VI issued the Papal Bull *Inter caetera* (or among other) divided trading and colonizing rights between Portugal and Spain (Castile), excluding other European nations such as England and Netherlands. The following year, Spain and Portugal signed the Treaty of Tordesillas. The New World was ripe for Catholic conversion and the Pope declared King Ferdinand of Spain apostolic vicar in the Indies.

---

74   Marshall Connolly, "A Very Brief History of Priestly Celibacy in the Catholic Church," *Catholic Online,* August 24, 2016. Retrieved September 29, 2020, from https://1ref.us/1e3.
75   My emphasis for "thus sayeth the Lord," the Papacy uses a "thus sayeth the blade."
76   Tim Roosenberg, "Daniel 11 Commentary," Islam and Christianity in Prophecy, 2019. Retrieved September 29, 2020, from https://1ref.us/1e4.

Chapter 10:
End-Time Divided Kingdoms

The French Revolution left France as a more atheistic power but not completely void of Catholicism. There are striking parallels between General Titus and Napoleon and their attitudes towards the temple and the Pope, respectively. Titus did not want the temple destroyed and gave orders to preserve it,[77] and Napoleon did not want to end the Papacy, so he tried to preserve it. An article by *Ministry Magazine* entitled, "Napoleon And The Pope—What Really Happened In 1798?"[78] points out the France Directory, and not Napoleon ordered General Berthier to capture the Pope. Hence, what we see here, Titus ending the prophecies of Imperial Rome (legs) parallels Napoleon starting the prophecies of End-Time Divided Kingdoms (toes).

The Papacy as head of a church-state system is, in essence, a theocratic state. The Catholic Church is just one of numerous theocratic state religious systems. The Puritans were not fleeing the Catholic state religion; they were fleeing the Anglican state religion in a Protestant nation. Islam is also a theocratic state system. Essentially, we have a theocratic state religion anytime the majority of religious views begin to subjugate minority religious views.

There are also state religions based on atheism—a non-theocratic belief system promoting secularism, evolution, and human reasoning. Often these secular state religions adopt policies prohibiting individual

---

77 The French Revolution left France as a more atheistic power but not completely void of Catholicism. There are striking parallels between General Titus and Napoleon and their attitudes towards the temple and the Pope, respectively. Titus did not want the temple destroyed and gave orders to preserve it, 8.
78 C. Ward, "Napoleon and the Pope—What Really Happened in 1798?" *Ministry Magazine,* 1978. Retrieved September 29, 2020, from https://1ref.us/1e5.

religious views. Prime examples of states who imprisoned or killed those who would not give up their religious beliefs include Revolutionary France, Nazi Germany, the Soviet Union, and Communist China.

Protestant America was different. Instead of a state-mandated belief system, the Founders recognized the freedom of individual conscience on these matters. While the idea of Separation of Church and State was deemed heretical in England, in 1634 Reverend John Lothropp, left the clergy in England to join the Puritans in Massachusetts. He was recorded to have proclaimed he found a "church without a bishop...and a state without a king." Nevertheless, around this same time, another minister, Roger Williams, began speaking out against the Puritans enforcing their religious beliefs by secular law. Williams was banished and set up the colony of Rhode Island where freedom of conscience was respected for all. Freedom of conscience ultimately led to the creation of the US Constitution which placed separation of church and state front and center. These tenets are undeniably under attack today.

"Congress shall make no law respecting an establishment of religion, or prohibiting the free exercise thereof; or abridging the freedom of speech, or of the press; or the right of the people peaceably to assemble, and to petition the government for a redress of grievances."[79]

While it is clear why Papal Rome would have its sights on America, a nation greatly blessed by God, this book will not attempt to suggest an in-depth interpretation for Daniel 11:40–45 verse by verse here. Still, the SDA Bible Commentary, Dr. Norman McNulty, and many others have excellent insight into these verses comprising significant end-time issues. (See appendix for a brief interpretation verse by verse.)

---

79 U.S. Constitution, Bill of Rights, Amendment I, National Archives. Retrieved November 3, 2020, from https://1ref.us/1fm.

Chapter 11:
Ellen White and Daniel 11

The Bible is the most instructive history that men possess. It came fresh from the fountain of eternal truth, and a divine hand has preserved its purity through all the ages. It lights up the far-distant past, where human research seeks vainly to penetrate. In God's word we behold the power that laid the foundation of the earth and that stretched out the heavens. Here only can we find a history of our race unsullied by human prejudice or human pride. Here are recorded the struggles, the defeats, and the victories of the greatest men this world has ever known. Here the great problems of duty and destiny are unfolded. The curtain that separates the visible from the invisible world is lifted, and we behold the conflict of the opposing forces of good and evil, from the first entrance of sin to the final triumph of righteousness and truth; and all is but a revelation of the character of God.[80]

The proposed interpretation for Daniel 11 in this book has been fleshed out using Scripture, proven methods of biblical interpretation, and detailed historical events and analysis. Other than in the Foreword, the Spirit of Prophecy has not been referenced, even though I could have undoubtedly filled every page with quotes from the Servant of God. Why, then, no quotes here, you might ask? Isn't that the best way to "prove" new interpretations of Scripture to Seventh-day Adventists? Not only does she have little to say in her writings directly referencing Daniel 11, but more importantly, the original reasoning for the study "Daniel from a Different

---

80 Ellen G. White, *Patriarchs and Prophets* (Washington, DC: Review and Herald Publishing Association, 1890), 596.

Direction" was for non-Seventh-day Adventists. Also, she, herself, would have wanted the Bible and not her writings to be the textbook.

Ellen G. White's Three Main References to Daniel 11

> The light that Daniel received from God was given especially for these last days. The visions he saw by the banks of the Ulai and the Hiddekel, the great rivers of Shinar, are now in process of fulfillment, and all the events foretold will soon come to pass.[81]

> The world is stirred with the spirit of war. The prophecy of the eleventh chapter of Daniel has nearly reached its complete fulfillment. Soon the scenes of trouble spoken of in the prophecies will take place.[82]

> We have no time to lose. Troublous times are before us. The world is stirred with the spirit of war. Soon the scenes of trouble spoken of in the prophecies will take place. The prophecy in the eleventh of Daniel has nearly reached its complete fulfillment. Much of the history that has taken place in fulfillment of this prophecy will be repeated. In the thirtieth verse a power is spoken of that 'shall be grieved, and return, and have indignation against the holy covenant: so shall he do; he shall even return, and have intelligence with them that forsake the holy covenant.' [Verses 31–36, quoted.][83]

Notice that Mrs. White connects the visions in chapters 8 and 9 (Ulai) and 10–12 (Hiddekah) as regarding the last days. The visions' final scenes are now in the process of fulfillment, and all the events foretold will soon come to pass. She indicates the final elements of Daniel 11 will be troublous and rapidly forthcoming. Finally, she indicates that the final scenes of this chapter will be "repeated."

Her statements here do not contradict the proposed interpretation of verses 23–29 in this book's previous pages. We have noted that Daniel 11 is a prophecy specifically for the last days. We have looked at parallel verses which depict scenes comparable to previous prophecies (not dual fulfillment, mind you). These passages help keep the interpretation on track by identifying similar or opposite elements. Also, she links Daniel

---

81 Ellen G. White, *The SDA Bible Commentary*, Vol. 4 (Washington, DC: Review and Herald Publishing Association, 1955), 1166.
82 Ellen G. White, *Testimonies for the Church*, Vol. 9 (Mountain View, CA: Pacific Press Publishing Association, 1909), 14.
83 Ellen G. White, *Manuscript Releases*, Vol. 13 (Silver Spring, MD: Ellen G. White Estate, 1990), 394.

10–12 with Daniel 8 and 9. In these chapters, we find Imperial Rome with a short description as the horizontal horn before it moves into Papal Rome with a longer, more detailed vertical horn description. A final note here, she mentions the Papacy in verse 30, "a power is spoken of." Some have indicated this as the rise of the Papacy, but it can also be seen as the Papacy in its full power and authority ready to "take action against the holy covenant." If this rendering is held, and Mrs. White gives no indication it is impossible, we can conclude that the Papacy's rise could have possibly occurred before verse 30. We will stop short of stating she confirmed the above elements of this new interpretation in verses 23–29, but again, her statements do not contradict the elements or interpretations stated here.

Mrs. White is silent on the Predominant Interpretation of Daniel 11:23–29

Earlier we looked at the predominant view which extends Imperial Rome from verses 20–29 regarding the Roman league with the Jews of 163 BC, the affair of Mark Anthony and Cleopatra, the Roman Civil War, and the Battle of Actium of 31 BC. However, after searching the online Ellen G. White Writings website and confirming through email correspondence with the White Estate, there are no direct quotations or implied references to these events.

I have been studying Mrs. White's writings for more than 25 years, especially her relation to Scripture. Early on I noticed several Scriptures that she never quoted, others that she would paraphrase. For some she used the marginal reading, and still others where she would quote from a version other than the KJV. All Bible translations contain an element of human error, yet what I noticed was she never referenced a text that was translated incorrectly. Mind you, she does not say, "the Scripture is in error," she just rephrases, uses the marginal reference, uses a newer translation, or simply does not use the text.

Example of Not Quoting: Mrs. White never quotes 1 John 5:7 in the KJV, **"For there are three that bear record in heaven, the Father, the Word, and the Holy Ghost: and these three are one."** This text, often called the "Johannine Comma"[84] was added to the Catholic Latin Vulgate by Erasmus after being accused of promoting Arianism and threatened with ex-communication if he did not add the text. The translators of the KJV accepted it from the Vulgate and used the text in their English translation. Yet, Mrs. White who believed in a trinitarian Godhead, instinctively, or better—supernaturally, knew not to use it!

---

84 "Johannine Comma," Theopedia, n.d. Retrieved September 29, 2020, from https://1ref.us/1e6.

Example of Paraphrasing: Jesus healing at the Pool of Bethesda. Mrs. White quotes directly from John 5:2,3, but stops the quote at verse 4. Instead of quoting, "**For an angel went down** at a certain season into the pool, and troubled the water: whosoever then first after the troubling of the water stepped in was made whole of whatsoever disease he had" she paraphrases, "At certain seasons the waters of this pool were agitated, and **it was commonly believed that this was the result of supernatural power**."

Example of Marginal Use: "These things have I spoken unto you in **proverbs**: but the time cometh, when I shall no more speak unto you in **proverbs**, but I shall shew you plainly of the Father."[85] Instead, she used "'These things have I spoken unto you in **parables**,' He said; 'but the time cometh, when I shall no more speak unto you in **parables**, but I shall show you plainly of the Father.' John 16:25, margin."[86]

Example of Newer Bible Versions: On John 13:10, she states, "Jesus had a lesson, deep, full, and significant: 'He that is washed needeth not save to wash his feet, but is clean every whit: and ye are clean, but not all. [KJV]' The true version reads, "He that is bathed needeth not save to wash his feet [RV]."[87] The lesson for us is not that there is a "true" Bible version versus a false Bible version, but for her, the "true version" is the one with the clearest, most understandable meaning and message.

Suffice to say, this author believes that Mrs. White may not have been comfortable with the interpretations regarding Imperial Rome of Daniel 23–29 of her day, and God, in His wisdom, saw fit to not give her light on these verses. Yes, as some have said, she may have not wanted to get into the middle of a dispute between her husband, James White, and Uriah Smith over the King of the North and the King of the South,[88] yet, she never wavered in giving the message God had for her in other areas.

The Great Controversy and Daniel 11:23–12:2

The proposed interpretation is easily seen in the example below and other writings:

> In the sixth century the Papacy had become firmly established. Its seat of power was fixed in the imperial city, and the bishop of Rome was declared to be the head over the entire church. Paganism had given place to the Papacy. The dragon had given to the beast "his

---

85   John 16:25 (KJV).
86   Ellen G. White, *The Ministry of Healing* (Mountain View, CA: Pacific Press Publishing Association, 1905), 430.
87   Ellen G. White, "The Lord's Supper and the Ordinance of Feet-Washing," *The Review and Herald* (July 5, 1898), para 6. Retrieved October 29, 2020, from https://1ref.us/1e7.
88   For more on these views see: David H. Thiele, "A Comparison and Contrast of James White and Uriah Smith on Daniel 11," n.d. Retrieved September 29, 2020, from https://1ref.us/1e8.

Ellen White and Daniel 11   91

power, and his seat, and great authority." Revelation 13:2. And now began the 1260 years of papal oppression foretold in the prophecies of Daniel and the Revelation. Daniel 7:25; Revelation 13:5–7. Christians were forced to choose either to yield their integrity and accept the papal ceremonies and worship, or to wear away their lives in dungeons or suffer death by the rack, the fagot, or the headsman's ax. Now were fulfilled the words of Jesus: "Ye shall be betrayed both by parents, and brethren, and kinsfolks, and friends; and some of you shall they cause to be put to death. And ye shall be hated of all men for My name's sake." Luke 21:16, 17. Persecution opened upon the faithful with greater fury than ever before, and the world became a vast battlefield. For hundreds of years the church of Christ found refuge in seclusion and obscurity. Thus says the prophet: "The woman fled into the wilderness, where she hath a place prepared of God, that they should feed her there a thousand two hundred and three-score days. Revelation 12:6.[89]

Below are the chapter headings of The Great Controversy with each verse in the sequence of Daniel 11:22–12:2 that would fall in her seminal work on the end time.

1. The Destruction of Jerusalem and 2. Persecution in the First Centuries

> 22 And with the arms of a flood shall they be overflown from before him, and shall be broken; yea, also the prince of the covenant.

3. The Great Apostasy (Mrs. White summarizes the extent of the full power of the Papacy on pages 49–54 and then reverts back to the beginning of the 1290/1260 years on page 54.

> 36 And the king shall do according to his will; and he shall exalt himself, and magnify himself above every god, and shall speak marvellous things against the God of gods, and shall prosper till the indignation be accomplished: for that that is determined shall be done.

> 37 Neither shall he regard the God of his fathers, nor the desire of women, nor regard any god: for he shall magnify himself above all.

---

89 Ellen G. White, *The Great Controversy* (Mountain View, CA: Pacific Press Publishing Association, 1911), 54.

38 But in his estate shall he honour the God of forces: and a god whom his fathers knew not shall he honour with gold, and silver, and with precious stones, and pleasant things.

39 Thus shall he do in the most strong holds with a strange god, whom he shall acknowledge and increase with glory: and he shall cause them to rule over many, and shall divide the land for gain.

23 And after the league made with him he shall work deceitfully: for he shall come up, and shall become strong with a small people.

24 He shall enter peaceably even upon the fattest places of the province; and he shall do that which his fathers have not done, nor his fathers' fathers; he shall scatter among them the prey, and spoil, and riches: yea, and he shall forecast his devices against the strong holds, even for a time.

25 And he shall stir up his power and his courage against the king of the south with a great army; and the king of the south shall be stirred up to battle with a very great and mighty army; but he shall not stand: for they shall forecast devices against him.

26 Yea, they that feed of the portion of his meat shall destroy him, and his army shall overflow: and many shall fall down slain.

27 And both of these kings' hearts shall be to do mischief, and they shall speak lies at one table; but it shall not prosper: for yet the end shall be at the time appointed.

28 Then shall he return into his land with great riches; and his heart shall be against the holy covenant; and he shall do exploits, and return to his own land.

29 At the time appointed he shall return, and come toward the south; but it shall not be as the former, or as the latter.

30 For the ships of Chittim shall come against him: therefore he shall be grieved, and return, and have indignation against the holy covenant: so shall he do; he shall even return, and have intelligence with them that forsake the holy covenant.

31 And arms shall stand on his part, and they shall pollute the sanctuary of strength, and shall take away the daily sacrifice, and they shall place the abomination that maketh desolate.

Ellen White and Daniel 11

> 32 And such as do wickedly against the covenant shall he corrupt by flatteries: but the people that do know their God shall be strong, and do exploits.

Chapters 4–14 on the Protestant Reformation:

4. The Waldenses, 5. John Wycliffe, 6. Huss and Jerome, 7. Luther's Separation From Rome, 8. Luther Before the Diet, 9. The Swiss Reformer, 10. Progress of Reform in Germany, 11. Protest of the Princes, 12. The French Reformation, 13. The Netherlands and Scandinavia, and 14. Later English Reformers

> 33 And they that understand among the people shall instruct many: yet they shall fall by the sword, and by flame, by captivity, and by spoil, many days.
>
> 34 Now when they shall fall, they shall be holpen with a little help: but many shall cleave to them with flatteries.
>
> 35 And some of them of understanding shall fall, to try them, and to purge, and to make them white, even to the time of the end: because it is yet for a time appointed.

15. The Bible and the French Revolution

> 40 And at the time of the end shall the king of the south push at him: and the king of the north shall come against him like a whirlwind, with chariots, and with horsemen, and with many ships; and he shall enter into the countries, and shall overflow and pass over.

Chapters 16–34 are not explicitly alluded to in Daniel 11.

35. Character and Aims of the Papacy (this is summary and expansion of the Papacy in the last days)

36. The Impending Conflict

> 41 He shall enter also into the glorious land, and many countries shall be overthrown: but these shall escape out of his hand, even Edom, and Moab, and the chief of the children of Ammon.
>
> 42 He shall stretch forth his hand also upon the countries: and the land of Egypt shall not escape.

37. The Scriptures a Safeguard

38. The Final Warning

43 He shall become ruler of the treasures of gold and of silver, and all the precious things of Egypt, and the Libyans and the Cushites shall follow in his train.

44a But news from the east and the north shall alarm him,

39. The Time of Trouble

44b and he shall go out with great fury to destroy and devote many to destruction.

45 And he shall pitch his palatial tents between the sea and the glorious holy mountain. Yet he shall come to his end, with none to help him

12:1ab At that time shall arise Michael, the great prince who has charge of your people. And there shall be a time of trouble, such as never has been since there was a nation till that time. (quoted GC 613; 635)

40. God's People Delivered

1c But at that time your people shall be delivered, everyone whose name shall be found written in the book.

2 And many of those who sleep in the dust of the earth shall awake, some to everlasting life, and some to shame and everlasting contempt. (quoted 637)

Chapters 41 and 42 are not explicitly alluded to in Daniel 11.

In sum, Mrs. White does not reference or endorse her time's predominant interpretation, or any of the interpretational views extending Imperial Rome from verse 23 to verse 29. Even so, she also did not openly endorse the proposed interpretation of verses 23–29, nevertheless what she does encourage is more and deeper study into Daniel 11. Nothing in this new proposal contradicts the Spirit of Prophecy, and the interpretation of this proposal matches the sections in the Great Controversy regarding the rise of the Papacy, the full power and control of Rome, and the Protestant Reformation.

Chapter 12:
Conclusion

This interpretation does so many things on so many levels. First, it gives an interpretation in a clear, concise, systematic manner, that is chronological and literal. Next, it enlarges and expands the prophecies of 2, 7, and 8–9; even so, it does not add elements that were not seen in the earlier prophecies. This will give teachers and presenters confidence, power, and enthusiasm in the message of Daniel 11. While this interpretation is innovative and different from previous positions on the Kings of the North and South, it does not remove any pillars of our faith. Instead, the position exults the sanctuary and Sabbath message while giving an interpretation void of any "perceived" Ellen White taint by those outside the Adventist Church. This could be precisely why she had nothing specific to say about the interpretation of Daniel 11.

It was never my intention to bring another position to Daniel 11. My purpose was simply to study Daniel's prophecies out for myself. Then I could make a different type of Bible study emphasizing each kingdom and what each of the four prophecies said about that kingdom instead of our usual chapter by chapter studies. My study was going to be titled "Daniel from a Different Direction," but instead of it being something for non-Adventists, it developed in a different direction for Adventists. While loving the study of the Bible and history, I feel that I am just an amateur in the areas of theology and history. While innumerable hours of diligent study and research has gone into this book, to be honest, I cannot explain some of the insights and concepts in this position other than God put them into my mind as I prayed and studied over these issues. It was only the Lord who could have done this.

I strongly believe we are hanging on by the toenails and the closing scenes will be rapid ones. I would like to reemphasize something that was stated earlier regarding our duty as priests of Jesus. God's New Testament people are a holy and royal priesthood of believers. Symbolically, in the Courtyard, we are justified and have 1) accepted Jesus who was sacrificed once for all, and 2) been baptized into his death and resurrection. We are now able to enter the Holy Place of the Sanctuary to spiritually perform the "continual/daily" duties of a priest 3) before the Altar of Incense with our personal and corporate prayers, 4) before the Table of Showbread through Bible study and devotions, and 5) before the Lampstand letting our light shine through our Fruit and Gift(s) of the Spirit. Finally, we are ministers at the curtain separating the Holy from the Most Holy Place 6) symbolically sprinkling the blood of Jesus by trusting in His merits as our only Sacrifice and High Priest to provide us mercy and give us the strength to keep His commandments. Thus, we emulate His character of love in our lives as He prepares us for glorification at His soon coming.

Now is the time for us to do our daily priestly duties in the sanctuary by praying, studying, and letting our light shine. Even so, let it be said of us, "And those who are wise shall shine like the brightness of the sky above; and those who turn many to righteousness, like the stars forever and ever."[90]

---

[90] Dan. 12:3.

Appendix A
Brief Verse by Verse Interpretation of Daniel 11

Introduction continued from Chapter 10 (Verse 1)

1 And as for me, in the first year of Darius the Mede, I stood up to confirm and strengthen him.

Years of 539–465 BC: Persia (Verse 2)

2 And now I will show you the truth. Behold, three more kings shall arise in Persia, and a fourth shall be far richer than all of them. And when he has become strong through his riches, he shall stir up all against the kingdom of Greece.

- 4 Persian Kings
  - Cyrus the Great 559–530 BC
  - Cambyses II 530–522 BC
  - Darius I 522–486 BC
  - Xerxes I 485–465 BC
- This rich, powerful fourth king is Xerxes I (the Greek name for Ahasuerus), Queen Esther's husband. He raised a huge army from forty different nations and attacked Greece around 480 BC.
- The Greek city-states began to band together to repel the Persian invasion.

Years of 331–301 BC: Greece and Alexander (Verse 3–4)

3 Then a mighty king shall arise, who shall rule with great dominion and do as he wills.

- Alexander and the Grecian Empire

4 And as soon as he has arisen, his kingdom shall be broken and divided toward the four winds of heaven, but not to his posterity, nor according to the authority with which he ruled, for his kingdom shall be plucked up and go to others besides these.
- On June 10 or 11, 323 BC in Babylon, Alexander died of malaria or typhoid fever combined with a drinking binge.
- "Divided to the four winds" between his generals in 301 at the Battle of Ipsus.
  - North—Lysimachus eastward in Thrace and Asia Minor
  - South—Ptolemy in Egypt and southern section of Asia Minor
  - East—Seleucus to the Indus River
  - West—Cassander in Macedonia and Greece
- "Not to his posterity" for 25 years Alexander's half-brother tried to keep the divisions together, but Alexander's only son and his Persian mother were poisoned in ca 310 BC by General Cassander.

Years of 301–188 BC: Hellenistic Seleucid and Ptolemy Dynasties (Verse 5–19)

5 "Then the king of the south shall be strong, but one of his princes shall be stronger than he and shall rule, and his authority shall be a great authority.
- "King of the South" located to the south of Palestine is Ptolemy I (Sotor) assisted "one of the princes" Seleucus I (Nicator) to regain the territories of Mesopotamia ca 312 BC and became a greater ruler than Ptolemy I ca 281 BC.

6 After some years they shall make an alliance, and the daughter of the king of the south shall come to the king of the north to make an agreement. But she shall not retain the strength of her arm, and he and his arm shall not endure, but she shall be given up, and her attendants, he who fathered her, and he who supported her in those times.
- "King of the North" located north of Palestine is now Antiochus II (Theos), in ca 253 BC who marries Bernice, the daughter of Ptolemy II (Philadelphus). They have a son, but separate and Antiochus II reconciles with his other wife and sister, Laodice.
- Antiochus II dies suddenly, possibly poisoned by Laodice. Laodice, then, had Bernice and her infant son killed.

7 And from a branch from her roots one shall arise in his place. He shall come against the army and enter the fortress of the king of the north, and he shall deal with them and shall prevail.

- ca. 246 BC Ptolemy III (Euergetes) invaded Syria in revenge for his sister Bernice and was victorious all the way to Mesopotamia and established Egyptian sea power.

8 He shall also carry off to Egypt their gods with their metal images and their precious vessels of silver and gold, and for some years he shall refrain from attacking the king of the north.
- ca. 239 BC Ptolemy III brought back enormous amounts of Egyptian treasures looted by the Persians but did not attack the Seleucid empire again.

9 Then the latter shall come into the realm of the king of the south but shall return to his own land.
- Seleucus I tried to march against Ptolemy III in 240 BC and regain the wealth lost but was defeated and turned back.

10 "His sons shall wage war and assemble a multitude of great forces, which shall keep coming and overflow and pass through, and again shall carry the war as far as his fortress.
- "[S]ons" Seleucus II, Seleucus III, and Antiochus III would carry on the war against Ptolemy IV (Philopater) in the Palestine region. In 219 BC Antiochus III marches to the "fortress" of Seleucia or port of Antioch on the Mediterranean sea.

11 Then the king of the south, moved with rage, shall come out and fight against the king of the north. And he shall raise a great multitude, but it shall be given into his hand.
- 217 BC at the Battle of Raphia, Ptolemy IV met Antiochus III's each with huge armies of around 60,000 infantry, 6,000 cavalry, and 100 elephants. Ptolemy IV soundly defeated Antiochus III.

12 And when the multitude is taken away, his heart shall be exalted, and he shall cast down tens of thousands, but he shall not prevail.
- After Ptolemy IV defeated Antiochus III at the Battle of Raphia, he instituted the Raphia Decree, placing himself on the level of the ancient Pharaohs, making himself a god, he put down the Egyptian Revolts, and finally, in 604, Ptolemy IV died of unclear circumstances.

13 For the king of the north shall again raise a multitude, greater than the first. And after some years he shall come on with a great army and abundant supplies.
- In 201 BC, Antiochus III invaded Palestine again. "After some years" refers to the 16 years between the Battle of Raphia and his second invasion giving him time to amass a great army and supplies.

14 "In those times many shall rise against the king of the south, and the violent among your own people shall lift themselves up in order to fulfill the vision, but they shall fail.
- One of those who rose against Ptolemy V (Epiphanes) was Rome who was violent and robbed the people as they conquered.

15 Then the king of the north shall come and throw up siegeworks and take a well-fortified city. And the forces of the south shall not stand, or even his best troops, for there shall be no strength to stand.
- Antiochus III captured Gaza from Ptolemy V in 201 BC, possibly captured Sidon, and made the Egyptian army surrender at the Battle of Panium 200 BC ending Ptolemaic control of Palestine.

16 But he who comes against him shall do as he wills, and none shall stand before him. And he shall stand in the glorious land, with destruction in his hand.
- "[S]hall do as he wills." The Romans who came against Antiochus III "shall do as he wills, and none shall stand before" Rome. And Antiochus III shall "stand in the glorious land, with destruction in his hand."

17 He shall set his face to come with the strength of his whole kingdom, and he shall bring terms of an agreement and perform them. He shall give him the daughter of women to destroy the kingdom, but it shall not stand or be to his advantage.
- In trying to conquer Egypt, Antiochus III (King of the North) made an agreement with the young Ptolemy V (King of the South) which included giving Antiochus's daughter Cleopatra I in marriage to Ptolemy V in Egypt. Cleopatra I turned against her father and gave up all ties to her ancestry in the Seleucid dynasty and later became the queen of Egypt and adopted the Ptolemy dynasty as her own.

18 Afterward he shall turn his face to the coastlands and shall capture many of them, but a commander shall put an end to his insolence. Indeed, he shall turn his insolence back upon him.
- Antiochus III attempted to extend his empire by invading Asia Minor and Greece but was stopped and routed in 191 BC by the Roman general Manius Acilius Glabrio.

19 Then he shall turn his face back toward the fortresses of his own land, but he shall stumble and fall, and shall not be found.
- Antiochus III was killed trying to plunder a pagan temple near Susa (187 BC) a year following the peace accords with Rome (188 BC); thus, he "stumbled and fell and was found no more." Rome is now

the dominating power and has subdued both the KON and the KOS in the Treaty of Apamea in 188 BC.

Years of 63 BC–AD 70: Imperial Roman Empire (Verses 20–22)

20 "Then shall arise in his place one who shall send an exactor of tribute for the glory of the kingdom. But within a few days he shall be broken, neither in anger nor in battle.
- Pompey laid siege to and conquered Jerusalem in 63 BC and levied high taxes on the Jews prompting Josephus to declare that Julius Caesar reduced the taxes by 20%. Pompey was soon after killed, not in battle, but by two friendly acquaintances paid by Ptolemy XIII to assassinate him so Ptolemy could win Julius Caesar's favor.

21 In his place shall arise a contemptible person to whom royal majesty has not been given. He shall come in without warning and obtain the kingdom by flatteries.
- Julius Caesar arose in Pompey's place. The Roman Senate had prohibited all generals when returning to Rome from military campaigns from crossing the Rubicon River with their armies. This was considered an act of insurrection against the Republic of Rome. Without warning, Julius Caesar did this in 49 BC and tried to obtain the kingdom by political ambitions and through his writings. He was brutally assassinated in a failed attempt to keep overall authority in the hands of the Roman Senate and not an emperor.

22 Armies shall be utterly swept away before him and broken, even the prince of the covenant.
- The power of Rome is seen in its crushing legions not only devouring nations around them, but more importantly being the power who through Pilate, issued a death decree, and carried it out, on Jesus, the Prince of the Covenant.
- The Gospel of Salvation was spread like wildfire to all the nations of the world within the first few centuries.

Years of 508–1215: Establishment of Church-State System in Europe (Verses 23–27)

23 And from the time that an alliance is made with him he shall act deceitfully, and he shall become strong with a small people.

- Starting at 476, after the fall of the Western Roman Empire the Papacy had to make temporary alliances with its barbarian neighbors in order to survive. The alliance with the Franks beginning in 508 would not only be stronger than all the rest but would remain steadfast until the time appointed of 1798.
- At this time because of the Barbarian invasions and Arianism, Catholicism was small but began to spread rapidly throughout southern, central, and western Europe through missionaries and with the sword of the Franks.

24 Without warning he shall come into the richest parts of the province, and he shall do what neither his fathers nor his fathers' fathers have done, scattering among them plunder, spoil, and goods. He shall devise plans against strongholds, but only for a time.

- In 533, the Papacy began the process of receiving a temporal dominion with the Byzantine Emperor giving the pope the city of Rome.
- Simony, the practice of buying and selling ecclesiastical privileges, church offices, or promotion, began as early as 498.
- The pope of Rome had to "devise plans" to be a temporal ruler using monastic establishments to spread spiritual rule throughout Europe and leverage against the Emperor who had the Bishop of Constantinople at his side.
- "But only for a time" is a significant phrase. The word time means "the time of an event." And the Papacy would engage in scattering plunder, spoil, and goods among those who honor them until the time of the end in 1798.

25 And he shall stir up his power and his heart against the king of the south with a great army. And the king of the south shall wage war with an exceedingly great and mighty army, but he shall not stand, for plots shall be devised against him.

- 535–554 The Gothic Wars with Byzantine General Narses (KOS) and an overwhelming force defeated the Ostrogoths again liberating Rome at the Battle of Taginae of 552 and vanquishing the remaining Ostrogothic army for good.
- As to "plots shall be devised against him," this can clearly be seen in the fact that Papacy initially supported the Arian Ostrogoths and also in the subsequent interplay between the popes, Ostrogoths, and the emperor.

26 Even those who eat his food shall break him. His army shall be swept away, and many shall fall down slain.

- None of the alliances with the Barbarian nations could give the Papacy the temporal power against Constantinople during this period. The Exarchate of Ravenna under the authority of the Byzantine emperor dominated the region. The populace of the peninsula had been devastated by war, famine, and disease. Also, the Papacy had lost control over papal elections. The Papacy would not gain the upper hand on Constantinople until 800 with the crowning of the French king, Charlemagne.

27 And as for the two kings, their hearts shall be bent on doing evil. They shall speak lies at the same table, but to no avail, for the end is yet to be at the time appointed.
- 711 Pope Constantine traveled to Constantinople to end a dispute over the Quinisext Ecumenical Council with Emperor Justinian II. However, the pope's real motive was the split over sacramental marriages. A compromise was reached where Pope Constantine gave ground on "Economia" or the handling, management, and disposition of the council, but he held firm on most papal concerns. It was truly a compromise borne in diplomatic speak between the two rival "kings" where many words were spoken but accomplished little towards ending the rift between the two parties.

28 And he shall return to his land with great wealth, but his heart shall be set against the holy covenant. And he shall work his will and return to his own land.
- After 756 and the establishment of the Papal States territories in the majority of the Italian Peninsula gave direct temporal sovereign rule to the Pope.
- In 787, the 2nd Council of Nicaea approved idol worship and declared that tradition superseded Scripture.

29 At the time appointed he shall return and come into the south, but it shall not be this time as it was before.
- The pope as KON with his Frankish armies attacked Constantinople, the KOS again. Charlemagne with sizable force attacked the Byzantine peripheral states of Venice and the Dalmatian coast. The Byzantines were not in a position to send a force to their aid. Additionally, the pope refused to acknowledge Irene as Byzantine Emperor in 797. In 811, a peace treaty was finally signed between Charlemagne and Byzantine emperor Michael I where the Byzantine Empire would accept Charlemagne as king of the Franks, and Charlemagne would give back the Dalmatian coast region.

30 For ships of Kittim shall come against him, and he shall be afraid and withdraw, and shall turn back and be enraged and take action against the holy covenant. He shall turn back and pay attention to those who forsake the holy covenant.
- Out of their Mediterranean Sea bases, Arab pirate raiders sacked Rome in 843, which caused the Papacy to withdraw and form the Italian League of Papal, Neapolitan, Amalfitan, and Gaetan ships to fend off the Arab pirates and winning the famous naval Battle of Ostia in 849.
- In 870, at the Fourth Council of Constantinople, the Covenant was again attacked with the sanctioning idolatry and veneration of Mary.

31 Forces from him shall appear and profane the temple and fortress, and shall take away the regular burnt offering. And they shall set up the abomination that makes desolate.
- At this point in time, the Papacy held all ecclesiastical authority in the Western Church. The pope's "forces" were the temporal powers in Europe, the increased focus of the inquisition beginning in the 1250s, and later with the Jesuit Order beginning in 1540
- At the Fourth Council of Lateran in 1215, it was ordered that parishioners must keep the annual reception of penance and the Eucharist. They also used the term "transubstantiation" to explain the Real Presence of Christ in the Eucharist. Through the Eucharist and the Sacraments, the Catholic church has removed the Daily/Continual sanctuary ministries of lay members. Congregants no longer study the Bible for themselves, pray directly to God, or witness to their neighbors.
- In AD 70, the Imperial Roman flags or standards with the iconic eagle were set up in the temple of Jerusalem commemorating their victory which was the abomination prophesied in AD 31 by Jesus. Likewise, starting around 1215 with the sanctions of its counsels, the Papacy harnessed the use of secular forces to enforce the church dogmas which were in direct contradiction to the teachings of the Apostles and of Scripture especially in the areas of the sanctuary which set up the Papal Roman abomination of desolation.

Years of 1215–1798: Protestant Revolution (verses 32–35)

32 He shall seduce with flattery those who violate the covenant, but the people who know their God shall stand firm and take action
- Those who violate the covenant are those who choose to accept tradition and church dogma over Scripture.

Brief Verse by Verse Interpretation of Daniel 11

- This "flattery" or smooth things can be seen in the praise the Mass in the Roman Missal which was produced in1570 and continued in use unchanged for 400 years.
- The Catholic church worked hand-in-hand with the Habsburg Dynasty against the Protestant Reformation overtly in Spain and Italy and likewise, covertly using the Jesuits in Central Europe.
- Shortly after the Third Council of Lateran, in 1209 the French military began the Albigensian or Cather Crusade which lasted for 20 years.

33 And the wise among the people shall make many understand, though for some days they shall stumble by sword and flame, by captivity and plunder.
- In 1553, Queen Mary I or "Bloody Mary" took the English throne, and many Protestants were exiled, imprisoned, burned at the stake, tortured, or punished in other ways. "Foxe's Book of Martyrs" records many accounts of persecution.

34 When they stumble, they shall receive a little help. And many shall join themselves to them with flattery,
- Many Catholics sympathizers in Protestant areas joined with the Protestants to avoid conflict. With the full authority of the pope and the Council of Trent, the church persecuted and burned at the stake millions who would not succumb to their edicts and dictates of the pope.
- At the Council of Trent in 1563 all previous beliefs were upheld and reinforced under penalty of death including tradition superseding Scripture, salvation was not by "faith alone", the Mass as a real sacrifice of Jesus, purgatory was real, indulgences were freely available for a price, the jurisdiction of the pope was universal, and initiated the Counter-Reformation.

35 And some of the wise shall stumble, so that they may be refined, purified, and made white, until the time of the end, for it still awaits the appointed time.
- recantation was used by some reformers to avoid death.
- "until the time of the end, for it still awaits the appointed time" is another specific reference to the time of the end in 1798.

Years of 1453–1798: Full Power and Authority of the Papacy (verses 36–39)

36 "And the king shall do as he wills. He shall exalt himself and magnify himself above every god, and shall speak astonishing things against the God of gods. He shall prosper till the indignation is accomplished; for what is decreed shall be done.

- The Papacy had reached the height of its power. He now headed the only Christian church-state system with the fall of Constantinople. He was able to make political rulers conform to their wishes by the threat of excommunication. He used his state power to persecute the Protestants. And finally, through his councils, edicts, he has attacked the holy covenant by controverting the plan of salvation by instituting the Eucharist, profaned and replaced the daily sanctuary service by instituting the rosary, prayers to Mary and the saints, forbid the reading and possession of the Bible, instituting a system of salvation by works, and finally changing God's commandants by removing the 2nd and allowing for image worship and replacing the 4th with Sunday worship. He will continue until 1798 when the indignation against him will reach its fill.

37 He shall pay no attention to the gods of his fathers, or to the one beloved by women. He shall not pay attention to any other god, for he shall magnify himself above all.

- Here we see the Papacy elevating tradition and councils over the Bible, the Word of God, and promoting celibacy. In the mid-16th century, Pope Pius V stated, "The Pope and God are the same, so he has all power in Heaven and earth."
- This *"god his fathers did not know"* refers to traditions, council canons, veneration of Mary, and papal bulls that have come in and replaced the Word of God.
- In 1074, Pope Gregory VII, champion of priestly celibacy, with his published encyclical, forbid the priests and clergy from marrying and command they stay celibate.

38 He shall honor the god of fortresses instead of these. A god whom his fathers did not know he shall honor with gold and silver, with precious stones and costly gifts.

- This *"god of fortresses"* can be seen in the temporal power of the pope not only with the Jesuits, Dominicans, and Papal Army but the powers of Catholic nations. Instead of using a "thus sayeth the Lord," the Papacy used a "thus sayeth the blade."
- Much of the money parishioners paid for indulgences went to pay for massive cathedrals adorned with gold, and precious stones of images of Mary and the Saints to be worshiped.

39 He shall deal with the strongest fortresses with the help of a foreign god. Those who acknowledge him he shall load with honor. He shall make them rulers over many and shall divide the land for a price.

Brief Verse by Verse Interpretation of Daniel 11 107

- "foreign god" could be Mary and her doing the CoRedemtrix with Jesus and the belief she was taken to heaven without sin.
- Distribution of land for a price can be seen in the church's property holdings throughout the world.
- In 1493, Pope Alexander VI issued the Papal Bull Inter caetera or "Among other" divided trading and colonizing rights between Portugal and Spain (Castile) excluding other European nations such as England and Netherlands. The following year, Spain and Portugal signed the Treaty of Tordesillas. The New World was ripe for Catholic conversion and the pope declared King Ferdinand of Spain apostolic vicar in the Indies.

Years 1798—2nd Coming of Jesus: Papal Power at the End of Time (verse 40–45, 12:1)

40 "At the time of the end, the king of the south shall attack him, but the king of the north shall rush upon him like a whirlwind, with chariots and horsemen, and with many ships. And he shall come into countries and shall overflow and pass through.
- In 1798, Revolutionary France took Pope Pius VI captive and exiled him. This ended the Papal rule during the medieval divided kingdoms and the 1260 and 1290-year prophecies that started in 508 with the crowning of Clovis.
- The Papacy has in these last days been resurrected in pronounce, universally respected, and mouthpiece of both the Catholic and Protestant churches. This began in 1929 with the Lateran Treaty when Italy gave the Papacy temporal power with the Vatican nation. The Vatican received diplomatic relations from nations all over the world including an ambassador from the United States in 1983. It will soon combine forces with the United States to reinforce its dogmas of the medieval period against the holy covenant.

41 He shall come into the glorious land. And tens of thousands shall fall, but these shall be delivered out of his hand: Edom and Moab and the main part of the Ammonites.
- In 2015, we witnessed Pope Francis standing in the well of the US Congress and his address the world at the United Nations. While this may not be the exact fulfillment of the prophecy regarding Papacy coming with power into Protestant lands, it is patently obvious where the trajectory to is headed in regard to a union of church and state.

- Edom, Moab, and the Ammonites were ancient relatives of the Jews. In the final days, when the full intentions of the Papacy will be revealed, many from the various Protestant churches will come out and take their stand with God's end-time people.

42 He shall stretch out his hand against the countries, and the land of Egypt shall not escape.
- The Papacy and the United States will work hand-in-hand to force the entire world to bow to Papal dogmas against God's covenant.

43 He shall become ruler of the treasures of gold and of silver, and all the precious things of Egypt, and the Libyans and the Cushites shall follow in his train.
- Papal authority and power will sweep the world over including groups of atheism, paganism, and Eastern religions.

44 But news from the east and the north shall alarm him, and he shall go out with great fury to destroy and devote many to destruction.
- The loud cry of the authentic Scriptural covenant message and God's true day of worship will lighten the world forcing all inhabitants to choose between standing with Michael and His people or keeping Sunday, the Papacy's counterfeit, pagan day of worship.

45 And he shall pitch his palatial tents between the sea and the glorious holy mountain. Yet he shall come to his end, with none to help him.
- Enraged, the Papacy will coerce the United States and the world to pass a death decree against Michael's people—Seventh-day Adventists and all other Sabbatarians who join them.
- Like in the time of Esther, just before the date the decree is to be carried out, the Papacy will come to its end.

Verse 12:1 is the conclusion of the prophecy of Chapter 11

1 "At that time shall arise Michael, the great prince who has charge of your people. And there shall be a time of trouble, such as never has been since there was a nation till that time. But at that time your people shall be delivered, everyone whose name shall be found written in the book.
- Probation closed on the Jewish nation in AD 34 when Stephen was stoned and Jesus stood up, pronounced the Jewish nation "guilty," and closed the court case in God vs the Jewish nation. When this final death on God's people falls, probation closes and Michael/Jesus will stand up, pronounce the Papacy church-state system "guilty" and close the court case in God vs the Papacy and her church-state system giving judgment in favor of God's Covenant keeping people.

Appendix B
The 21 Ecumenical Councils[1]

by Karl Keating

6/1/1993

Aside from the first general gathering of the bishops of the Church—the Council of Jerusalem, which occurred around AD 50 (Acts 15) and which is usually not counted as an ecumenical council—there have been 21 ecumenical or general councils of the bishops of the Catholic Church. (The Eastern Orthodox Churches recognize the first seven as ecumenical councils.)

A council is recognized as ecumenical once its works are approved by a pope. The pope does not need to attend a council for it to be an ecumenical council. The earliest councils were held in the East, and the reigning popes usually sent legates to represent them. Later these popes approved the decrees of the councils, thereby verifying that they were ecumenical councils.

Some councils, such as Ephesus, have been mainly doctrinal in their work; others, such as Vatican II, have been mainly pastoral. Doctrinal definitions are capable of being promulgated infallibly; pastoral decisions, although binding, are not subject to infallibility.

1. Nicaea I
325
Pope Sylvester I, 314–335
Emperor Constantine, 306–337
Decisions: Condemned Arianism, which denied the divinity of Christ (elements of Arianism have reappeared in our own time); defined the

---

1 Keating, "21 Ecumenical Councils."

consubstantiality of the Father and the Son; fixed the date for Easter; began formulation of Nicene-Constantinopolitan Creed.

2. Constantinople I
381
Pope Damasus I, 366–384
Emperor Theodosius, 379–395
Decisions: Recondemned Arianism; condemned Macedonianism, which denied the divinity of the Holy Spirit; completed the formulation of the Nicene-Constantinopolitan Creed.

3. Ephesus
431
Pope Celestine I, 422–432
Emperor Theodosius II, 408–450
Decisions: Condemned Nestorianism, which denied the unity of the divine and human in Christ; defined that Mary is the Mother of God (Theotokos), a doctrine denied by the Nestorians and by most of today's Protestants; condemned Pelagianism, which held that man could earn his own salvation through his natural powers.

4. Chalcedon
451
Pope Leo the Great, 440–461
Emperor Marcian, 450–457
Decisions: Condemned Monophysitism (also called Eutychianism), which denied Christ's human nature.

5. Constantinople II
553
Pope Vigilius, 537–555
Emperor Justinian I, 527–565
Decisions: Condemned the Three Chapters, writings tainted by Nestorianism and composed by Theodore of Mopsuestia, Theodoret of Cyr, and Ibas of Edessa.

6. Constantinople III
680
Pope Agatho, 678–681
Emperor Constantine IV, 668–685
Decisions: Condemned Monothelitism, which held Christ had but one will, the divine (this heresy arose as a reaction to the monophysite heresy); censured Pope Honorius I for a letter in which he made an ambiguous

but not infallible statement about the unity of operations in Christ (an episode commonly used by anti-Catholic writers as an argument against papal infallibility, but for the real meaning, see Catholicism and Fundamentalism, pages 227–229).

7. Nicaea II
787
Pope Hadrian I, 772–795
Emperor Constantine VI, 780–797
Decisions: Condemned iconoclasm (which was mainly confined to the East), a heresy that held that the use of images constituted idolatry; condemned Adoptionism, which held that Christ was not the Son of God by nature but only by adoption, thereby denying the hypostatic union.

8. Constantinople IV
869
Pope Hadrian II, 867–872
Emperor Basil, 867–886
Decisions: Recondemned Adoptionism; deposed Photius as patriarch of Constantinople, thereby ending the Photian Schism, but this did not completely remove disaffections between the West and the East (in 1054 came the final break, when the Eastern Orthodox Churches broke away from unity with Rome).

9. Lateran I
1123
Pope Callistus II, 1119–1124
Emperor Henry V, 1105–1125
Decisions: Confirmed the Concordat of Worms (1122), in which the Pope and Emperor sought to end the dispute over investiture (the attempt by the secular powers to assume authority in appointing bishops; this was a main source of Church/state friction during the Middle Ages).

10. Lateran II
1139
Pope Innocent II, 1130–1143
Emperor Conrad III, 1138–1152
Decisions: Ended a papal schism by antipope Anacletus II; reaffirmed baptism of infants; reaffirmed the sacramental nature of the priesthood, marriage, and the Eucharist against Medieval heretics; decreed that holy orders is an impediment to marriage, making the attempted marriage of a priest invalid.

11. Lateran III

1179

Pope Alexander III, 1159–1181

Emperor Frederick Barbarossa, 1152–1190

Decisions: Regulated papal elections by requiring a two-thirds vote of the cardinals (see in this issue the article by Canon Francis J. Ripley, page 27); condemned Waldensianism and Albigensianism, a form of Manichaeanism (an ancient heresy that held that matter is evil; Albigensians opposed the authority of the state and of the Church, opposed the sacrament of matrimony, and practiced ritual suicide; despite these tenets, many anti-Catholics believe Albigensianism was the continuation of "real Christianity" during the Middle Ages and was a forerunner of Protestantism).

12. Lateran IV

1215

Pope Innocent III, 1198–1216

Emperor Otto IV, 1209–1215

Decisions: Ordered annual reception of penance and the Eucharist; used the term "transubstantiation" to explain the Real Presence of Christ in the Eucharist; adopted further canons against the Albigensians.

13. Lyons I

1245

Pope Innocent IV, 1243–1254

Emperor Frederick II, 1220–1250

Decisions: Excommunicated and deposed Frederick II for heresy and crimes against the Church.

14. Lyons II

1274

Pope Gregory X, 1271–1276

Emperor Rudolf I, 1273–1291

Decisions: Effected only temporary union of the Eastern Churches with the Roman Church; promulgated regulations for conclaves.

15. Vienne

1311

Pope Clement V, 1305–1314

Emperor Henry VII, 1308–1313

Decisions: Suppressed the Knights Templars; issued decrees on the reform of morals.

16. Constance
1414
Popes Gregory XII, 1406–1415
Emperor Sigismund, 1410–1437
Decisions: Ended the Great Schism, which involved three rival claimants to the papacy (see in this issue the article by Canon Francis J. Ripley, page 27); opposed the teachings of John Wycliffe, who taught sola scriptura, denied the authority of the pope and bishops, denied the Real Presence of Christ in the Eucharist, and wrote against penance and indulgences; condemned as a heretic John Huss, who denied papal authority and taught wrongly about the nature of the Church and who was burned at the stake in 1415 (in 1457 his followers established what became known commonly as the Moravian Church, which was the first independent Protestant church).

17. Florence
1438–1443
Pope Eugene IV, 1431–1447
Emperors: Albert II, 1438–1439
Frederick III, 1440–1493
Decisions: Reaffirmed papal primacy against claims of conciliarists that an ecumenical council is superior to a pope; approved reunion with several Eastern Churches, but the reunion was only temporary.

18. Lateran V
1512–1517
Popes Julius II, 1503–1513
Leo X, 1513–1521
Emperor Maximilian I, 1493–1519
Decisions: Opposed erroneous teachings about the soul; reaffirmed the doctrine of indulgences; restated the relationship between popes and ecumenical councils; on the eve of the Protestant Reformation, failed to inaugurate an authentic and thoroughgoing reform of the Church, inadvertently helping Protestantism.

19. Trent
1545–1549, 1551–1552, 1562–1563
Popes Paul III, 1534–1549
Julius III, 1550–1555
Pius IV, 1559–1565
Emperors Charles V, 1519–1558
Ferdinand I, 1558–1564

Decisions: Affirmed Catholic doctrines against the errors of the Protestant Reformers; reaffirmed teachings on the role of the Bible and Tradition, grace, sin, justification by faith (but not by "faith alone"), the Mass as a real sacrifice, purgatory, indulgences, jurisdiction of the pope; initiated the Counter-Reformation; reformed the clergy and morals; promoted religious instruction; ordered the establishment of seminaries for the future training of priests.

20. Vatican I
1869–1870
Pope Pius IX, 1846–1878
Decisions: Defined papal infallibility and primacy; condemned errors regarding the relationship between faith and reason (the council was cut short by war, its work to be taken up again by Vatican II).

21. Vatican II
1962–1965
Popes John XXIII, 1958–1963
Paul VI, 1963–1978
Decisions: Issued pastoral documents on the renewal and reform of the Church, intending the make the Church more effective in dealing with the contemporary world.

Appendix C
The Continual Sanctuary Ministry

Hebrews 9:1–5 The Earthly Holy Place
> Now even the first covenant had regulations for worship and an earthly place of holiness. For a tent [or tabernacle] was prepared, the first section, in which were the lampstand and the table and the bread of the Presence [or the presentation of the loaves]. It is called the Holy Place. Behind the second curtain was a second section[of the tabernacle] called the Most Holy Place, having the golden altar of incense (technically, located in the Holy Place compartment, but with its sweet aroma flowing into and filling the Most Holy compartment) and the ark of the covenant covered on all sides with gold, in which was a golden urn holding the manna, and Aaron's staff that budded, and the tablets of the covenant. Above it was the cherubim of glory overshadowing the mercy seat.

What was "Continual" or done "Daily" in the Sanctuary?
The regular priests were to continually provide the following:
- In the Holy Place of the Sanctuary
    - Bread on the Table of the Presence[91]
    - Pure, beaten olive in the Seven-branch Lampstand[92]
    - Burning incense upon the Altar of Incense[93]
- In the Courtyard
    - The daily sacrifice of two lambs of the first-year day by day[94]

---
91 Exod. 25:30.
92 Exod. 27:20.
93 Exod. 30:8.
94 Exod. 29:38.

- Burnt offerings at the door of the tabernacle[95]
- Meat offerings with a tenth part of an ephah of fine flour, ½ I the morning and ½ in the evening[96]

The High Priest continually provided the following:

- Bear the names of the children of Israel in the breastplate of judgment upon his heart when going into the holy place[97]
- Wear a breastplate of judgment the Urim and the Thummim[98]
- Wear a plate of pure gold on the forehead, and grave like the engravings of a signet, HOLINESS TO THE LORD[99]

How the Sanctuary is Transgressed

It became great, even as great as the Prince of the host. And the regular burnt offering was taken away from him, and the place of his sanctuary was overthrown. And a host will be given over to it together with the regular (continual/daily) burnt offering because of transgression, and it will throw truth to the ground, and it will act and prosper. Then I heard a holy one speaking, and another holy one said to the one who spoke, "For how long is the vision concerning the regular burnt offering, the transgression that makes desolate, and the giving over of the sanctuary and host to be trampled underfoot?" And he said to me, "For 2,300 evenings and mornings. Then the sanctuary shall be restored to its rightful state."[100]

High Priest (Mediator): Represents Jesus[101]

- Transgressed through confession to church priests

Altar of Sacrifice: Represents Jesus substitutionary death on the cross[102]

- Transgressed through the Mass where the wine and bread become the literal body and blood of Jesus who is sacrificed every Sunday. Also, transgressed in the use of fermented wine resulting from decay.

---

95   Exod. 29:42.
96   Lev. 6:20.
97   Exod. 28:29.
98   Exod. 28:30.
99   Exod. 28:38.
100 Dan. 8:11–14.
101 Heb. 8:1.
102 John 1:29.

The Continual Sanctuary Ministry   117

Laver: Represents Baptism by immersion symbolizing the death, burial and resurrection of Jesus[103]

- Transgressed through sprinkling and infant baptism.

Lampstand: Represents Holy Spirit who interprets the Bible and convicts of sin[104]

- Transgressed through tradition and ecclesiastical counsels interpreting scripture; defining sin as mortal (a grave matter, done with full knowledge, and with deliberate consent) and venial sins (a sin that does not have all three elements for mortal sin)

Table of Showbread: Represents the Father and the Son who are the bread of life and are seated on the throne[105]

- Transgressed through the Pope claiming to be God on earth and Mary (Co-Redemtrix) is equal

Altar of Incense: Represents Prayers of the saints mingled with Jesus prayers[106]

- Transgressed through prayers to Mary and the Saints

Ark of the Covenant with the Ten Commandments: Represents God's character of love and mercy[107]

- Transgressed through removing the 2nd commandment prohibiting the worship of idols
- Transgressed through splitting the 10th commandment into two in order to preserve the "10" for the number of commandments
- Transgressed through changing the 4th Commandment from Sabbath to Sunday

Jesus entered the Most Holy Place in the Heavenly Sanctuary on October 22, 1844 at the end of the 2300-day prophecy. The counterfeit sanctuary system was completely set up by that time and continues to this day. The body of this book dealt with Catholic councils prior to 1798, but within a few years the deadly wound was on the mend devising plans to make more attacks on the true sanctuary.

In 1854, Pope Pius IV elevated the status of Mary. As stated by the International Marian Association, "Mary's Immaculate Conception,

---

[103] Rom. 6:3.
[104] Rev. 4:5.
[105] John 6:35; Matt. 4:4.
[106] Rev. 8:4.
[107] James 1:23, 25.

along with her Divine Motherhood, makes appropriate her unique cooperation in the redemptive work of Christ."[108] "REDEMPTORIS MATER: On the Blessed Virgin Mary in the life of the Pilgrim Church" was an entire Catholic encyclical on Mary issued by Pope John Paul II in 1987. The document states emphatically, "Mary's mediation is intimately linked with her motherhood. It possesses a specifically maternal character, which distinguishes it from the mediation of the other creatures who in various and always subordinate ways share in the one mediation of Christ, although her own mediation is also a shared mediation."[109]

In his 2003 encyclical during the "Year of the Rosary," Pope John Paul II states, "If we wish to rediscover in all its richness the profound relationship between the Church and the Eucharist, we cannot neglect Mary, Mother and model of the Church. In my Apostolic Letter Rosarium Virginis Mariae, I pointed to the Blessed Virgin Mary as our teacher in contemplating Christ's face, and among the mysteries of light I included the institution of the Eucharist. Mary can guide us towards this most holy sacrament, because she herself has a profound relationship with it."[110]

Salvatore M. Perrella, called by many in the Catholic Church as an expert in dogma and Mariology, describes Mary's role in redemption this way, "She herself, the first of the redeemed, receives this grace which, in a singular fashion, associates her with Christ's Redemption and gives her the function of manifesting it and fostering its effectiveness."[111]

These actions after 1844 were enacted predominately through the Papacy speaking in ex-cathedra place Mary squarely in the most holy place of the sanctuary they created. Daniel 11:38 states, "A god whom his fathers did not know he shall honor with gold and silver, with precious stones and costly gifts."

The true Sanctuary in Heaven has Jesus ministering his blood before the throne from His single sacrifice dispensing grace and mercy on behalf of His Covenant Keeping People.

In the counterfeit Catholic sanctuary, we find the pope as the head of the priesthood dispensing grace through the sacraments and sacrificing over and over Jesus' real body and blood. Mary, as co-redemptrix, accepts our prayers and devotions while dispensing mercy and fostering the effec-

---
108 "The Role of Mary in Redemption," International Marian Association, January 1, 2017. Retrieved September 30, 2020, from https://1ref.us/1e9.
109 Pope John Paul II, *"Redemptoris Mater,"* March 25, 1987. Retrieved September 30, 2020, from https://1ref.us/1ea.
110 Pope John Paul II, "Encyclical Letter *Ecclesia de Eucharistia,"* April 17, 2003. Retrieved September 30, 2020, from https://1ref.us/1eb.
111 Salvatore M. Perrella, "Mary's Cooperation in Work of Redemption," EWTN Global Catholic Network (July 2, 1997): 9. Retrieved September 30, 2020, from https://1ref.us/1ec.

How God Feels About His Sanctuary

> Son of man, do you see what they are doing, the great abominations that the house of Israel are committing here, to drive me far from my sanctuary? But you will see still greater abominations.[112]
>
> Then he said to me, 'Have you seen this, O son of man? Is it too light a thing for the house of Judah to commit the abominations that they commit here, that they should fill the land with violence and provoke me still further to anger? Behold, they put the branch to their nose. Therefore I will act in wrath. My eye will not spare, nor will I have pity. And though they cry in my ears with a loud voice, I will not hear them.'[113]
>
> Now the glory of the God of Israel had gone up from the cherub on which it rested to the threshold of the house. And he called to the man clothed in linen, who had the writing case at his waist. And the Lord said to him, "Pass through the city, through Jerusalem, and put a mark on the foreheads of the men who sigh and groan over all the abominations that are committed in it." And to the others he said in my hearing, "Pass through the city after him, and strike. Your eye shall not spare, and you shall show no pity."[114]

As priests of the Lord, we are to continually pray, study the Scriptures and witness. As last day People of the Covenant we are to "sigh and groan over all the abominations that are committed in (His sanctuary)" as we witness in patience, love, and kindness. Nevertheless, it is God's work to send out His angels to do His strange work of passing through the earth and striking those committing abominations in His sanctuary. The stone crushes the feet and toes of the image and kingdom of God becomes a great mountain, fills the whole earth, and the people of His covenant possesses the kingdom forever.

---

112   Ezek. 8:6.
113   Ezek. 8:17–18.
114   Ezek. 9:3–5.

Bibliography

Allies, Thomas William. "Justinian." *The Formation of Christendom* VI (n.d.). https://1ref.us/1d2 (accessed September 27, 2020).

Barclay, W. *De potestate papae: an, et quatenus in Reges et Principes seculares jus et imperium habeat* (1609). https://1ref.us/1hj (accessed January 7, 2021).

Bollman, C. "Why the Year 538?" *Ministry Magazine* (1931). https://1ref.us/1d3 (accessed September 27, 2020).

Bingham, Steven. *Image of God the Father in Orthodox Theology and Iconography*. Oakwood Publication, 1995.

Cairns, E. *Christianity Through the Centuries: A History of the Christian Church*. Grand Rapids, MI: Zondervan, 1954.

Campbell & Satelmajer. *Here We Stand: Luther, the Reformation, and Seventh-day Adventism*. Nampa, ID: Pacific Press Publishing Association, 2017.

"Canons and Decrees of the Council of Trent." Wikisource (November 24, 2016). https://1ref.us/1di (accessed September 30, 2020).

Connolly, Marshall. "A Very Brief History of Priestly Celibacy in the Catholic Church." Catholic Online (August 24, 2016). https://1ref.us/1e3 (accessed September 29, 2020).

"Decrees of Justinian Declaring John, Bishop of Rome to be Chief Bishop of All the Churches [AD 533], The." (n.d.). https://1ref.us/1dp (accessed September 27, 2020).

Denzinger, Heinrich. "Sources of Catholic Dogma," English translation, older numbering (n.d.). https://1ref.us/1dg (accessed September 27, 2020).

"East-West Schism." Wikipedia, The Free Encyclopedia (2020). https://1ref.us/1d7 (accessed September 29, 2020).

"First Council of Constantinople." Wikipedia, The Free Encyclopedia (2020). https://1ref.us/1d5 (accessed September 29, 2020).

"Fourth Lateran Council: 1215 Council Fathers." Papal Encyclicals Online (December 12, 2017). https://1ref.us/1df (accessed September 27, 2020).

Gane, Roy. "A Suggested Interpretation of Daniel 11:1–21." American Ministry Magazine (n.d.). https://1ref.us/1cy (accessed September 27, 2020).

—. "Methodology for the Interpretation of Daniel 11:2–12:3." *Journal of the Adventist Theological Society* 27, no. 1 (2016): 317–319. https://1ref.us/1d0 (accessed October 29, 2020).

Gottheil, R., & S. Krauss. "Cyprus." *Jewish Encyclopedia*. 1906. https://1ref.us/1dr (accessed September 27, 2020).

Hardy, F. W. "Clovis and the Year AD 508." (2016). https://1ref.us/1dm (accessed October 29, 2020).

"Inquisition." History.com (2017). https://1ref.us/1du (accessed September 29, 2020).

"Jesuit Order Established." History.com (2010). https://1ref.us/1dv (accessed September 29, 2020).

"Johannine Comma." Theopedia (n.d.). https://1ref.us/1e6 (accessed September 29, 2020).

Keating, K. "The 21 Ecumenical Councils." Catholic Answers.com (December 5, 2019). https://1ref.us/1dd (accessed September 27, 2020).

Lechler, Gotthard Victor. *John Wycliffe and His English Precursors*. Religious Tract Society, 1904.

Lightfoot, J. "Didache." Early Christian Writings.com (2001). https://1ref.us/1dc (accessed September 27, 2020).

"List of Protestant Martyrs of the English Reformation." Wikipedia, The Free Encyclopedia (2020). https://1ref.us/1dz (accessed September 29, 2020).

Loughlin, James Francis. "Pope St. Agapetus I." *Catholic Encyclopedia* 1, edited by Charles Herbermann. New York: Robert Appleton Company, 1907.

Mann, Horace Kinder. "Pope John II." *Catholic Encyclopedia* 8 (1913). Wikisource. https://1ref.us/1do (accessed September 29, 2020).

Martin, Malachi. *The Keys to this Blood: Pope John Paul II Versus Russia and the West for the Control of the New World Order*. New York: Touchstone, 1990.

Mathisen, R. "Clovis, Anastasius, and Political Status in 508 C.E.: The Frankish Aftermath of the Battle of Vouille." *In The Battle of Vouillé, 507 CE: Where France Began*. Berlin/Boston: De Gruyter, 2012. https://1ref.us/1db (accessed October 29, 2020).

McNulty, Norman. *Commentary on the Book of Daniel: Practical Living in the Judgement Hour*. Coldwater, MI: Remnant Publishing, 2019.

Mutschlechner, M. "The Struggle for People's Souls—the Habsburgs and the Counter-Reformation." The World of Habsburgs (n.d.). https://1ref.us/1dy (accessed September 29, 2020).

Perrella, Salvatore M. "Mary's Cooperation in Work of Redemption." EWTN Global Catholic Network (July 2, 1997). https://1ref.us/1ec (accessed September 30, 2020).

Pope John Paul II. "Encyclical Letter *Ecclesia de Eucharistia*." (April 17, 2003). https://1ref.us/1eb (accessed September 30, 2020).

—. "*Redemptoris Mater*." (March 25, 1987). https://1ref.us/1ea (accessed September 20, 2020).

"Pope Nicholas I." Wikipedia, The Free Encyclopedia (2020). https://1ref.us/1d9 (accessed September 29, 2020).

"Pope Vigilius." Catholic Answers.com Encyclopedia (February 22, 2019). https://1ref.us/1d8 (accessed September 27, 2020).

Reason, A. "Sincere Lies and Creative Truth: Recantation Strategies During the English Reformation." *Journal of History and Cultures* 1 (2012). https://1ref.us/1e0 (accessed September 29, 2020).

"Role of Mary in Redemption, The." International Marian Association (January 1, 2017). https://1ref.us/1e9 (accessed September 20, 2020).

Roosenberg, Tim. "Daniel 11 Commentary." Islam and Christianity in Prophecy (2019). https://1ref.us/1e4 (accessed September 29, 2020).

Saint Gregory & E. Brehaut. *History of the Franks*. New York: Octagon Books, 1965. https://1ref.us/1dl (accessed October 29, 2020).

Santillana, Giorgio de. "Recantation of Galileo (June 22, 1633)." In *The Crime of Galileo*. Chicago: Chicago University Press, 1955. https://1ref.us/1e1 (accessed September 29, 2020).

"Secrets of the Sanctuary." Amazing Facts, *Inside Report* (2018). https://1ref.us/1dw (accessed September 29, 2020).

Shaw, R. *Papal Primacy in the Third Millennium*. Huntington, IN: Our Sunday Visitor Publications, 2000. https://1ref.us/1dh (accessed September 27, 2020).

Sorenson, C. Seventh-day Adventist Bible Conference (1919). https://1ref.us/1d4 (accessed October 29, 2020).

Spitzer, J. "Taxing Time." My Jewish Learning.com. https://1ref.us/1d1 (accessed September 27, 2020).

Stackpole, Robert. "Why Do We Call Mary 'Mother of Mercy.'" The Divine Mercy (January 16, 2016). https://1ref.us/1dx (accessed September 29, 2020).

Staples, Tim. "The Assumption of Mary in History." *Catholic Magazine Online* (August 12, 2019). https://1ref.us/1dt (accessed September 29, 2020).

Strong's Lexicon. *Blue Letter Bible*, n.d. https://1ref.us/158 (accessed October 29, 2020).

"Synod of Laodicea (4th Century)." New Advent.org (n.d.). https://1ref.us/1de (accessed September 27, 2020).

Tanner, N. P., ed. "Second Council of Nicaea—787 A.D." In *Decrees of the Ecumenical Councils*. Washington, DC: Georgetown University Press, 1990. https://1ref.us/1dq (accessed September 27, 2020).

Thiele, David H. "A Comparison and Contrast of James White and Uriah Smith on Daniel 11." Daniel 11 Prophecy Home (n.d.). https://1ref.us/1e8 (accessed September 29, 2020).

Thiessen, Gesa Elsbeth. *Theological Aesthetics: A Reader*. Grand Rapids, MI: William B. Eerdmans Publishing Company, 2005.

U.S. Constitution. Bill of Rights. National Archives. https://1ref.us/1fm (accessed November 3, 2020).

Volkmann, H. "Antiochus III the Great." *Britannica*, 2019. https://1ref.us/143 (accessed September 27, 2020).

Ward, C. "Napoleon and the Pope—What Really Happened in 1798?" *Ministry Magazine* (1978). https://1ref.us/1e5 (accessed September 29, 2020).

White, Ellen G. *Great Controversy, The*. Mountain View, CA: Pacific Press Publishing Association, 1911.

—. "The Lord's Supper and the Ordinance of Feet-Washing." *The Review and Herald* (July 5, 1898). https://1ref.us/1e7 (accessed October 29, 2020).

—. *Manuscript Releases*, Vol. 13. Silver Spring, MD: Ellen G. White Estate, 1990.

—. *Ministry of Healing, The*. Mountain View, CA: Pacific Press Publishing Association, 1905.

—. *Patriarchs and Prophets*. Washington, DC: Review and Herald Publishing Association, 1890.

—. *SDA Bible Commentary, The*, Vol. 4. Washington, DC: Review and Herald Publishing Association, 1955.

—. *Testimonies for the Church*, Vol. 9. Mountain View, CA: Pacific Press Publishing Association, 1909.

Wylie, J. A. *The Papacy Is the Antichrist: A Demonstration*. Edinburgh: George M'Gibbon, 1888. https://1ref.us/1dk (accessed September 27, 2020).

Other Media Bibliography

"Byzantine Empire AD 527." Map, Wikimedia Commons (2020). https://1ref.us/1d6 (accessed October 29, 2020).

"Christendom." Map, Wikipedia, The Free Encyclopedia (2020). https://1ref.us/1dn (accessed September 29, 2020).

"Europe AD 476." Map, Wikimedia Commons (2019). https://1ref.us/1da (accessed October 29, 2020).

"Ostia" by Raphael. Painting. Wikimedia Commons. https://1ref.us/1ds (accessed September 29, 2020).

"Protestant Reformation." Map of Religions in Europe, Wikimedia Commons. https://1ref.us/1e2 (accessed October 29, 2020).

TEACH Services, Inc.
P U B L I S H I N G

We invite you to view the complete
selection of titles we publish at:
www.TEACHServices.com

We encourage you to write us
with your thoughts about this,
or any other book we publish at:
info@TEACHServices.com

TEACH Services' titles may be purchased in
bulk quantities for educational, fund-raising,
business, or promotional use.
bulksales@TEACHServices.com

Finally, if you are interested in seeing
your own book in print, please contact us at:
publishing@TEACHServices.com

We are happy to review your manuscript at no charge.

www.ingramcontent.com/pod-product-compliance
Lightning Source LLC
Chambersburg PA
CBHW071219160426
43196CB00012B/2347